GOD'S
MAN
IN IRAQ

A CENTURY FOUNDATION BOOK

GOD'S MAN IN IRAQ

The Life and Leadership
of Grand Ayatollah Ali al-Sistani

Sajad Jiyad

Library of Congress Cataloguing-in-Publication Data Available from the publisher upon request.

Manufactured in the United States of America

Cover design by Jamal Saleh
Text design by Cynthia Stock

God's Man in Iraq: The Life and Leadership of Grand Ayatollah Ali al-Sistani
Sajad Jiyad

ISBN 978-0-87078-566-5 (paperback)
ISBN 978-0-87078-567-2 (e-book)
ISBN 978-0-87078-568-9 (Arabic edition)

Contents

About Author

Sajad Jiyad is a fellow at Century International and director of the Shia Politics Working Group. An Iraqi political analyst based in Baghdad, he is the managing director of Bridge, an Iraqi nongovernmental organization and consultancy focused on development projects for young people. Sajad's main focus is on public policy and governance in Iraq. He is frequently published and cited as an expert commentator on Iraqi affairs. Sajad's educational background is in economics, politics, and Islamic studies.

Acknowledgments

This book is part of a project on Shia politics that was made possible by the generous support of the Henry Luce Foundation, which enabled a multi-year research effort, and of the Carnegie Corporation of New York and the Open Society Foundations, which made it possible to see this work to its conclusion.

The board of trustees and my colleagues at The Century Foundation (TCF), led by Chairman Bradley Abelow and President Mark Zuckerman, have created the space for Century International to extend its commitment to innovative policy research. Century International's Advisory Board provided critical guidance and support: thanks to Lina Attalah, Melani Cammett, Mona Fawaz, Michael Wahid Hanna, and Marc Lynch. Former Luce program director Toby Volkman helped conceive the Shia politics project.

This biography benefited from feedback given by members of Century International's Shia Politics Working Group. Their research on Shia politics in Iraq, based on years of fruitful and challenging discussion and fieldwork, has been collected in a separate volume titled *Shia Power Comes of Age* (2023), also published by Century International.

The reviewers who generously gave their time—Marsin Alshamary, Toby Dodge, Shamiran Mako, and Babak Rahimi—provided extremely useful comments and suggestions that made this book much sharper than earlier drafts. Eamon Kircher-Allen did an immense job with the editing, turning dense and obfuscated writing into clearer, intelligible prose. The foreword by Juan Cole is a rich assessment of Ayatollah Ali al-Sistani and I am grateful for his endorsement.

This book would not have been possible without the encouragement and support of Century International director Thanassis Cambanis, who created a platform for this research, backed the premise of this book, provided critical comments during the writing, and gave me a continuous push to turn my incomplete thoughts into a proper book.

Several other people too numerous to recall here, including dear friends in Baghdad, Najaf, Qom, and London, have over the years helped inform my work by challenging my views on Sistani and Iraqi politics, opening up their contacts and resources, reading through earlier summaries and drafts, and providing critical evaluation of the concept of this book.

So much of the information relating to Sistani himself has come from scholars, politicians, and intellectuals—in Najaf, Karbala, Baghdad, Qom, Mashhad, Beirut, and London—whose conversations with me over two decades provided the basis for understanding Sistani's personality. I owe them all a debt of gratitude for sharing their knowledge and views, and for trusting me with firsthand accounts of interactions with Sistani that would otherwise never have been revealed.

Many thanks are due to my long-suffering family, particularly my wife Fatima and my mother Donia, who have endured my months and years away from them researching, writing, and working, with immeasurable patience. It is to them that I dedicate this book, a small token of my appreciation for all that they have done for me.

As is customary, any errors in the manuscript are mine alone.

—*Sajad Jiyad*
August 4, 2023

Foreword

By Juan Cole

The addled plan of the George W. Bush administration to carry out regime change in Iraq by overthrowing the secular, socialist Ba'ath Party in 2003 went wrong in all the ways that could be foreseen, and some that could not. The United States caught a break, however, in that the spiritual leader of the country's Shia majority, Ayatollah Ali al-Sistani, exhibited a rare wisdom. Sistani was no passive player and did not hesitate to challenge the Americans in dramatic ways on matters of principle. He was convinced, however, that the U.S. occupation would eventually end and that if the Shia played their cards deftly, they would inherit the government of Iraq. He eminently deserves this pathbreaking study by Sajad Jiyad.

Sistani, born in eastern Iran, came to the Shia shrine city of Najaf in Arab Iraq in the early 1950s. Najaf is the burial place of the Prophet Mohammed's cousin and son-in-law Ali ibn Abi Talib, the first Shia Imam and fourth Sunni caliph, who was assassinated there in 661. Faithful Shia believe that one in the line of Ali, Muhammad al-Mahdi or the rightly guided messiah, would someday return to restore the world to justice. A shrine grew up around Ali's tomb and clerics gradually established the preeminent Shia seminaries there in the medieval period. In modern times, most Arab Shia have followed the lead of the grand ayatollah in Najaf, whom the laity are expected to follow on matters of religious law. Sistani acceded to that position in the 1990s.

When Bush's viceroy in Iraq, Paul "Jerry" Bremer, announced in June 2003 that he would appoint a committee to write a new constitution, Sistani issued a sharp rebuke in the form of a fatwa, or considered legal opinion. A constitution, he said, must spring from the will of the Iraqi people, implicitly citing Jean-Jacques Rousseau's *The Social Contract*. Sistani insisted that an elected constituent assembly must draft the constitution, which should then be submitted for a national referendum. Bremer is said not to have known who Sistani was, and to have asked dismissively, "Can't we get a different fatwa from some other ayatollah?" Since Shia clerical authority has hierarchies, it was sort of like asking whether we could get an encyclical from some other pope.

In November 2003, when the American Coalition Provisional Authority was collapsing in the face of Iraqi opposition, Bremer declared, after consultations in Washington, that the Bush administration would sponsor "caucus-based" elections, which was a transparent attempt to choose a small elite electorate and to shoehorn into power some figure favored by the United States. Sistani called, in January 2004, for mass demonstrations in favor of one-person, one-vote democratic elections. He also wanted UN oversight. Washington was said to have been miffed. Thousands of protesters came out in Baghdad, and then in Basra. The ayatollah had made his point, and Bush and Bremer backed down with alacrity.

In April 2004, after Bremer had attempted to have the young dissident Shia cleric Muqtada al-Sadr arrested, a massive revolt broke out. Sadr's militia, the Mahdi Army (which anticipated the near advent of their messiah as signaled by the fall of their country to foreign troops), took over police stations and even Coalition military bases throughout the south. A force of U.S. Marines battled them in the city of Najaf. Neither the United States nor the Mahdi Army could win such a fight outright, and ultimately an end to the battles was negotiated through Sistani.

When Sistani had heart problems that summer, he went to London for treatment. I was told by U.S. military insiders that they were approached, in Sistani's absence, by other high-ranking clerics in Najaf, asking the United States to take down the Mahdi Army, whom these scholars viewed as undisciplined ruffians who threatened those same clerics. The U.S. military was delighted to comply, and fighting again broke out in Najaf. I was afraid that the Americans would bomb the shrine of Ali, sacred to Shia, where Sadr had taken refuge, and I warned against the U.S. campaign in my widely read blog and in the *Washington Post*. I was contacted by U.S. military spokesmen who were clearly puzzled at my vehemence. I now understand that they thought they had gotten the go-ahead from Sistani's colleagues and were on the side of the angels.

Sistani, of course, did not agree with his colleagues. When he heard what was going on, he got up from his sick bed in London and flew to Kuwait, making his way overland to Basra. From there, he called on all Shia to simply walk into Najaf. The faithful eagerly obeyed him, despite the dangerous battles in the shrine city, and as masses of noncombatants flooded into the town's narrow streets, the fighting subsided, since neither side wanted to be blamed for massacring innocent civilians. At the time, I compared Sistani's action to Mahatma Gandhi's tactics of nonviolent noncooperation. The shrine of Ali was thus saved, avoiding a mass Shia uprising against the United States.

Once Bush had bowed to several of Sistani's demands, the UN appointed veteran Algerian diplomat and former foreign minister Lakhdar Brahimi to shepherd the electoral process, which led to open elections in January 2005. In the meantime, Sistani had insisted that all the major Shia parties run on a single ticket, the United Iraqi Alliance (UIA), since he was aware that the Shia held the majority.

The UIA received more than 50 percent of the votes, and so was able to form a government. This elected parliament also functioned as a constituent assembly charged with drafting the constitution, which took on a Shia cast, as Sistani had envisioned.

As Jiyad shows in this book, Sistani eschewed the theory of Ruhollah Khomeini that, in the absence of the imam, the clerics should rule. He believed, rather, that clerics should intervene only when the "structure of society" was at stake, as with the drafting of a constitution or the framework for elections. He felt that even this role for the clerics of setting guardrails could only be carried out if the people accorded them sufficient authority to do so. He tried to forbid sectarian faction-fighting but was not always given the obedience by the laity that he was owed in theory. And in 2006, at the height of the Sunni–Shia civil war in Baghdad, he withdrew from any public role for a while in protest. In 2011, the United States finally withdrew, and as Sistani had foreseen, they left behind an Iraqi government in which Shia power predominated.

In 2014, the so-called Islamic State group took over the north and west of Iraq, chasing the rebuilt Iraqi Army out of Mosul. In the aftermath, the Iraqi Army completely collapsed, and Baghdad, Najaf, and Karbala seemed vulnerable to the militant Islamic State extremists. Sistani issued a fatwa calling upon Iraqi young men to arise to fight the enemy. Although his spokesmen later attempted to clarify that he meant for them to join the Iraqi Army (which for all intents and purposes no longer existed), most Iraqi Shia understood the fatwa as calling for the establishment of Shia militias to take on the Islamic State. A plethora of such forces, known as the Popular Mobilization Units (PMUs), were formed and went to the battlefield. Some of them, however, attracted funding and training from the Iranian Revolutionary Guards Corps. Still, the PMU fighters played an important role in the defeat of the Islamic State, and they formed political parties, becoming pro-Iran players in Iraq's perpetually deadlocked politics.

The grand ayatollah's legacy is not without blemishes. He was likely too insouciant in 2003 about the dangers of a tyranny of the Shia majority. It is not clear that his jurisprudence can accommodate the full liberty of all Iraqis, including women and gays. The militias he summoned in 2014, whether it was his intention or not, have become a standing danger to what shreds of Iraqi democracy remain. Still, Sistani undeniably helped shape post-Ba'ath Iraq in crucial ways, standing up to the more authoritarian plans of the American occupiers while calling on the faithful to remain calm when things were going their way. He declined power for himself and his colleagues, preferring to assert moral authority instead. As Jiyad argues, he implicitly laid an intellectual foundation for Iraqis to combine the best of their Enlightenment and Islamic heritages in forging a modern Iraq, accepting the principle of popular sovereignty. He was capable of the grand gesture and almost Gandhian tactics of nonviolent opposition. He denounced sectarian violence but was not always able to forestall it. He crafted a Shia parliamentary majority that has remained in power ever since. When Baghdad and the Shia south lay supine before murderous advancing Islamic State minions, he inspired patriotism in the youth and summoned volunteers to defend the country from this menace. His sense of humanity often transcended the political and religious traditions in which he was steeped, and one hopes that will be his last, best legacy to Iraq.

Juan Ricardo Cole is a public intellectual, prominent blogger and essayist, and the Richard P. Mitchell Collegiate Professor of History at the University of Michigan.

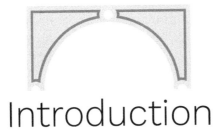

Introduction

Iraq's recent history, from the turn of the twentieth century until the present, is marked by upheaval, with very few years of stability. From the struggles to form an independent state to the emergence of a republic and to the fight for freedom from dictatorship, Iraq has been a nexus for debates on nationalism and ethnic and religious identity. At various points, there has been a strong interaction between religious and political authority, at the heart of which have been the most senior leaders in Shia Islam.[1] Since regime change in 2003, the most consequential of these leaders has been Grand Ayatollah Ali al-Sistani. Sistani has wielded tremendous informal power, but very little is known or written about him. This book aims to shed more light on the persona and politics of a figure revered by millions of people inside Iraq and abroad.

Sistani's primary role is that of a *marja taqlid* (literally, the source of emulation, singular marja, plural *maraji*), essentially an expert in Islamic law whose views and rulings are a source of religious authority for his followers. When necessary, he gives views on political matters or intervenes using his religious authority to effect political outcomes. In this regard, while Sistani may view himself solely as a religious figure, his position and actions mean there are political aspects to his role.

Sistani is an Iranian citizen who has lived in Iraq for more than seventy years.[2] While it may sound strange that a non-Iraqi has had such an important role in Iraqi politics, Sistani's religious authority is transnational and his devotion to Iraq has seen him persevere despite the tough conditions throughout the decades, because he believes he has a duty of care to his followers and the people of Iraq in general.

The vast majority of maraji in history have been limited to issuing religious opinions or jurisprudence on daily matters relevant to the faithful, and have not engaged with political matters that concern governance of society at large. Sistani and a small number of other maraji have been able to assert influence on a larger scale, and have intervened on a national or international level well beyond their communities.[3] But even when compared to this small group, Sistani's role and the scale of his impact are unparalleled. He has a preeminence among his peers that is exceedingly rare, he exerts political influence that the maraji usually cannot or do not, and his *marja'iyya*—the network of clerics, practices, and institutions of the marja—is unique in its size and scope.

Sistani is arguably the most influential Shia clerical authority since the early Safavid era (1501–1629 C.E.) because of his success in consolidating authority in multiple spheres at once: religion, politics, and international recognition. With his persistent and understated style, Sistani has laid out a vision for Shia religious leadership that I describe as "communal leadership," in contrast to Khomeini's model of direct clerical rule in Iran. Sistani's model still centers religion and clerical thinking in the daily life of adherents, but positions religious authority outside the state; Sistani created a template for how clerics could have influence over politics and state while remaining outside it—a model of religious activism (or Shia Islamism, if you will) that harnesses faith into public life, but in a manner markedly different from Iran's theocracy. The former Iranian supreme leader, Ayatollah Ruhollah Khomeini, used the concept of *wilayat al-faqih*, or the "guardianship of the jurist," to justify direct clerical rule—a clerical state. In contrast, Sistani has built a long record based on *iradat al-ummah*, or the will of the people. Sistani uses iradat al-ummah as a rationale for a communal leadership, in which clerics lead their adherents on those matters that fall outside the scope of state power, and maintain the primacy of the people's right to choose their governments. This communal leadership model has allowed Sistani to exert power and influence beyond the Shia population in Iraq and helped generate national political consensus.

When considering what type of authority Sistani exerts and how his role can be viewed when assessing the recent political history of Iraq, it is helpful to refer to the concepts of two eminent sociologists to help frame the discussion. First, Max Weber explains that authority is power accepted as legitimate by those subjected to it, and conceptualizes three types of authority: charismatic, traditional, and rational-legal.[4] Charismatic authority reflects the power to move others to action and mobilize them utilizing force of personality. As we shall see, Sistani certainly possesses this type of authority. He also possesses traditional authority through his marja'iyya, which can be considered inherited in some ways; and rational-legal authority (a type of institutional capacity), as confirmed in Iraq's Shia Endowment Law of 2005 and in the textbooks of Shia jurisprudence. Sistani is thus in the unique position of concurrently exerting legitimate authority through multiple channels. This analysis supports the view that, in addition to being a religious leader, he is a political figure.

Second, Pierre Bourdieu explains that, while capital, in his broader definition of it, comes principally in three forms (economic, cultural, social), a fourth—symbolic—is exercised when people do not designate the effects of capital as being due distinctly to one of the three principal forms.[5] As the notable historian and scholar of Iraq Toby Dodge explains:

Economic capital, the power to deploy financial resources is straightforward. Social capital comes from the extent of an actor's networks and associates, [in Bourdieu's words] "the size of the network of connections he can effectively mobilise." Cultural capital is central to Bourdieu's argument that culture has a stratifying power within society. The fourth and most important type of capital is symbolic capital and symbolic power. And it is the struggle for symbolic power within Iraq's political field that is the main explanatory focus of this paper. Symbolic capital has the ability to legitimize power relations. Those who wield symbolic capital—writers, teachers, and journalists, for example—have the ability to shape and legitimize perceptions of the social order . . . . Symbolic power comes from the ability to manipulate symbolic systems. Symbolic systems deliver individual cognition, communication and societal differentiation.[6]

Bourdieu's thoughts on the political economy of religion are that it is still a relevant institution in modern society and that "spiritual politics" have a role to play. This understanding makes a study of Sistani inherently political, given the symbolic capital he holds and the spiritual politics he engages in. But because Sistani has not made explicit his political ideology, it is left to others to assess it and find the most appropriate frameworks and concepts in which to place his practices.

For comparative purposes, it is relevant to note that Sistani's authority, and Shia clerical rule in general, resemble that of other hierarchical religious structures. For example, consider the role of the Pope for Catholics around the world, and the patriarchs of Eastern Orthodox churches such as the Greek Orthodox, Assyrian Church of the East, and Russian Orthodox churches.[7] All these figures fit into similar structures of authority, and enjoy vast power over their communities. Where Sistani's authority differs, though, is his influence on politics; further, his informal power has had a greater impact than that of other religious leaders.

To make this study more readable and to keep it focused on Sistani's role in politics, I narrowed the scope so that there is only very brief mention of his religious views and jurisprudential method, the history of the marja'iyya as an institution, details about the operation of the *hawza* (the religious seminary which trains students in Islamic sciences), explanations of how mujtahids (experts in Islamic law qualified to issue religious rulings) and maraji arise, and some aspects of the history of Iraq and Najaf in particular. But these subjects do provide context to Sistani's marja'iyya and his political interventions in Iraq, so readers should consult other published works that give further insights.[8]

Sistani himself has not described his political ideology nor published any work that explains his rationale or his views on the political roles of the maraji.[9] He does not grant interviews where he details his political thought, and only makes limited public comment on urgent political issues. Analyzing his actions, interventions, and statements gives an understanding of his approach. The primary source material for this study is the statements and rulings issued by Sistani and his office, the Friday prayer speeches delivered by his representatives in Karbala, the writings and comments of people close to Sistani, and the remarks and observations of politicians, clerics, and foreign diplomats, among others, who have met with Sistani. This is supported by secondary sources, other materials concerning Sistani and the marja'iyya in general, and my own analysis based on my experiences. Sistani's official website, sistani.org, and those of the shrines in Karbala, are good reference points, particularly the official biography on Sistani's site.[10]

Writing about a living figure of tremendous authority is a daunting task, and when assessing the life of Sistani there are several considerations to take into account. One of these is the fact Sistani is a religious authority whose instructions and guidance are followed by tens of millions of people around the world and whose role is viewed as an extension of divine leadership. Another is that Sistani is difficult to access, very little exists about his life before 2003, and even after it is mostly limited to official statements, making his political views much more challenging to assess than they should be, given his important role in Iraq. Also, writing as objectively as possible, on a figure whom this author respects immensely, when combined with the necessity of casting a critical eye on Iraqi politics and leaders, is no mean feat. This work aims to describe Sistani's political role as a marja and not to provide a full biography or give an exhaustive account of Shia political ideology.

As the first chapter describes, Sistani's marja'iyya adopts a policy of opacity, which makes researching and analyzing Sistani challenging. My interest in Sistani began in 2002 during the build-up to the invasion of Iraq, and I sought to understand what Sistani's position was in Iraq and would be after the war. In the twenty years since then, I have endeavored to collect as much information as I can about Sistani and dedicated many of my visits to Najaf to understanding how his marja'iyya operates. I have spoken to several of Sistani's students, clerics in Najaf and Qom, Iran who are familiar with Sistani's approach to politics, and politicians who have interacted with Sistani. These meetings and interviews provided much of the source material for this book, particularly anecdotes, and Sistani's views and thinking. Nearly all the information I received in these meetings and interviews was given in confidence and I have respected the requests for anonymity in this work.

This study is composed of four parts, the first giving a background on what the role of the maraji has been in politics, assessing their political authority, and why the marja'iyya is a closed institution. The second gives a short biography of Sistani and proceeds to document his political interventions from 2003 onwards. The third part analyzes Sistani's views and actions, in an effort to describe his political ideology. The final part is a conclusion looking at Sistani's legacy and its major criticisms, and the future of the marja'iyya after Sistani.

This work is the first of its type and it is hoped that this contribution will give readers a clearer picture of Sistani's philosophy and why he has been so important to Iraq. In my view, Sistani—by all the measures traditionally applied to assess an Ayatollah's stature—is the most influential marja to ever emerge from Najaf and his legacy will have an impact on Iraq and Shia Muslims for generations to come.

Religious Authority
in Shia Islam

There are two important discussions on religious authority that must occur before assessing the role of Sistani. These discussions allow us to understand the conditions and limitations under which he operates. Sistani is one link in a chain of Shia religious leaders that goes back over a millennium and, particularly in Najaf, there are strong traditions and expectations of how a marja is supposed to act.

Role of the Marja in Politics

Authority in Shia Islam, in all its forms, lies with the Prophet Mohammed and the twelve Imams, who are the inheritors of the Prophet's authority and knowledge. There have been critical debates throughout the centuries on the religious authority and political governance of the first eleven Imams and their representatives during their lifetimes, which stem from the doctrine of Imamate. For our interests here, we are focused on authority after the major occultation of the Twelfth Imam al-Mahdi began (941 CE), and specifically on the holders of authority rather than the topic of divine authority itself.[1] Due to the messianic Imam's concealment and inaccessibility, the role of religious leadership was gradually filled by the clerics who, based on rational and traditional evidence, asserted that they were his indirect deputies until his return.

For most of the history of Islam, the focus of *ijtihad* (the intellectual reasoning used to derive rulings in Islamic law) has been on personal religious affairs. But over the course of human development, ijtihad has also expanded to consider societal affairs. This same march of progress transformed the clerics from mostly local maraji to a sophisticated transnational network of clerical authority. It is no coincidence that Shia political jurisprudence developed whenever scholars interacted more with the state, as recognized religious authorities. Since the Shia have always been a minority of Muslims and rarely held political power, the maraji mostly avoided, in the words of scholar Hamid Mavani, the "challenge of providing pragmatic and practical guidance on state governance. Consequently, they felt no pressure or urgency to develop a state theory that conformed to Islam's textual sources."[2]

Since 941, Shia clerics have been the exclusive holders of religious authority in Shia Islam, and with the last three centuries, that role has been exercised specifically by the maraji.[3] While having a single supreme marja, the primus inter pares, has never been a necessity, for some periods of history there has been such a guide. In the modern context, the marja'iyya is the transnational system of religious authority and the network that represents the marja. The hawza is what produces the individuals ready to become maraji and provides the basis for the networks—it is the hierocracy. While the religious authority of the maraji dates back to 941, the marja'iyya as an institution evolved more recently, from the nineteenth century onwards.[4] Though Najaf has been the high seat of the hawza in this later period, other cities such as Baghdad, Karbala, and Hilla have all had earlier periods of primacy.[5] The last eighty years have seen a trend of institutionalization in the hawza and in the marja'iyya in order to keep pace with technology and globalization.

The path to becoming a marja is a long one; it requires decades of study and teaching in the hawza, and even then it depends on other factors difficult to assess or quantify by outsiders. Because clerics are free to try to become maraji and there is no elected head of Shia Islam in the way the Pope is elected in Catholic Christianity, several religious authorities may exist at the same time. Each marja retains the right to issue religious rulings or political views—though they may conflict with their peers—and no marja has the right to strip or block the authority of another marja. Thus, religious authority of the maraji is not solely concentrated in the hands of an individual. The fact that several maraji may exercise religious authority simultaneously leads to two broad outcomes from this overlap: disagreement and conflict or cooperation and accommodation, the latter of which is largely what has occurred in history.

The role of the maraji in politics is framed by a prior argument—the argument about whether Islam prescribes a particular form of government. The sources of Islamic law make it clear that they do not stipulate any one system. Rather, the chief concern of Islamic law is with governments being just and establishing an egalitarian society. That means democracy, theocracy, autocracy, and other forms of government can be legitimate if they serve this purpose. The next question is whether governments need to be Islamic in the absence of a divinely appointed leader. The majority of scholars do not view it as necessary for governments to be Islamic; it is a choice for people. Some scholars believe establishing Islamic governments should be prohibited, as only the infallible Imam is able to act in accordance with divine authority. Other scholars on the opposing end, such as Ayatollah Ruhollah Khomeini (d. 1989), believe governments must be Islamic and societies should strive to establish such governments.

This then presents us with two separate historic views on the role of the maraji in politics. One view, the predominant one, is that the maraji's scope of power and authority was circumscribed to community affairs (al-umur al-hisbiyah), which, in the words of

Mavani, "includes such functions as issuing legal opinions on jurid-
ical issues, implementing the penal code (hudud) and discretionary
penalties (ta'zir), inviting people to righteousness and discouraging
them from committing abominable acts, instituting congregational
prayers (especially the Friday prayer), supervising endowments and
collecting religious dues, and having limited authority over people
and properties (e.g., a discretionary mandate over children, orphans,
people of unsound mind, endowments, and unclaimed property)."[6]
As Shia Islam became the official state religion of Iran with the Safavid empire in 1501, the maraji began to take on more authority. This
led to Muhaqiq Karaki (d. 1533) and Muqaddas Ardabili (d. 1585),
among others, to consider the question of a marja's political mandate
and authority.[7]

This development laid the ground for the second view of the
authority or guardianship of the jurist, better known as wilayat
al-faqih, first posited systematically by Mulla Ahmad al-Naraqi
(d. 1829). The religious jurist—the marja—is seen as being a guardian for society, and more attuned to its interests than politicians. This
view gave the marja broad authority over society, including political
matters—not necessarily to be the ruler, but to ensure governments
did not contravene Islam.

The twentieth century brought much debate on constitutionalism, as some maraji sought to limit the monarch's authority. Ayatollah
Muhammad Hussain Naini (d. 1936) was the main proponent of the
supervisory role of a council of maraji over the state, without being
directly involved in government. The most powerful argument for
direct rule of the maraji was made by Khomeini from 1970 onward.
He extended the role of the marja as the Imam's indirect deputy with,
in the words of Mavani, "implementing the Islamic legal rulings and
serving as the public's guardian and custodian."[8] The supervisory
view evolved, eventually specifying a single marja (later, proponents
of this view held that it need not be a marja, and a qualified cleric

would suffice) as the ruler of the Islamic state; this is the current form of government in Iran. The supervisory role philosophy is still the minority view among the maraji today, with the majority not advocating for the direct rule of clerics and instead taking a nuanced position composed of elements from both views.

Some observers seek to frame the differences between the two main views on the role of the maraji as a full-on dichotomy between quietist and activist. But the scholar Mohammad R. Kalantari notes that this "distinction misunderstands both Shi'i political doctrine and the contemporary political history of the Middle East."[9] Today, the major schools of thought on the role of the maraji in politics are the Najafi school (inaccurately labeled quietist by most Western scholars), to which Sistani belongs, and the school of wilayat al-faqih al-mutlaqa (meaning the "absolute" guardianship of the jurist; this school is inaccurately labeled the school of Qom). The Najafi school limits the marja to an advisory role or provides a more active one contingent upon the people's demands and approval. Wilayat al-faqih al-mutlaqa, on the other hand, gives one or several maraji the right to rule as an extension of indirect divine authority.[10] Those are the theoretical viewpoints. But the maraji are involved in politics in other ways, not overtly, and it is this network effect that means most maraji are politically active in some form and not apathetic. In fact, no major marja today advocates for the maraji to be completely apolitical. Therefore, it seems that the context, conditions, opportunities, and threats that the maraji face help decide if they play a more or less active political role.

An alternative way of framing the two approaches can be through using the terms "communal leadership" to reflect the Najafi tradition in which religious authority informally participates in politics and is advisory rather than used to govern; and "direct clerical rule" as the approach wilayat al-faqih adopts when it comes to politics, whereby high-ranking clerics adopt formal positions in the state and exercise their authority to govern.

The Marja'iyya as a Closed Institution

"Our system is nonsystematic." This is the description one hears when asking hawza insiders how the marja'iyya operates and what its institutional processes are. This description does not mean the marja'iyya does not have a system, just that it is not systemized in the corporate or bureaucratic sense, and gives the appearance of being informal and uncodified. It is not entropy or disorder, but the result of a centuries-long tradition that has evolved to give and protect the autonomy of Shia clerical authority.

This non-systemization is composed of two parts. First is the maintenance of a decentralized hierarchy with informal processes and a pedagogical model that largely does not rely on formal examinations and certification, which makes it difficult to replicate in an external environment. Second is the opacity to the workings of the hawza and the marja'iyya so that only those within it and granted sufficient access are able to influence them.

The marja'iyya and hawza have a deliberate policy of maintaining opacity, for several reasons. The first is to avoid infiltration of the hawza by state agents and outsiders and to avoid the possibility of disruption from within. The second is preventing co-optation by the state and maintaining independence from it, using the highly developed techniques of jurisprudence that are difficult to teach and, for nonspecialists, to understand. The third is upholding a thousand-year-old tradition of religious authority that has proven successful and avoids being undermined by unnecessary reforms. The fourth reason for opacity is to keep the weaknesses of the hawza and marja'iyya hidden from opponents, and thus make it less likely those weaknesses will be exploited.

The marja'iyya is not an open institution, the laity cannot assess it with full transparency or much hold it to account. How a marja is chosen, how the marja'iyya operates, the finances it controls, its policies, its network, and its internal mechanisms of management are not available for inspection.[11] Historically, there was no real pressure or incentive to change this model, because the maraji mostly focused on providing religious guidance and the small amounts of taxes collected and services provided were not significant enough to attract state attention.[12] However, as the marja'iyya expands its capabilities and resources, as it has done under Sistani, establishing public services and generating many funds through investment, there will be more questions from the laity and from governments on how the marja'iyya conducts its affairs. In Iraq, corruption is a reality that affects most institutions and services, so it is logical to expect that corruption affects the marja'iyya in some way. Additionally, as the political influence of the marja'iyya has grown, so have the questions about how Sistani reached his status, what his influence is composed of, and how accountable his interventions are.

It is unlikely that the marja'iyya will voluntarily opt for more transparency, but the power of the marja is predicated upon people's acceptance and trust. A mujtahid may be eminently qualified to become a marja, but without followers he remains a teacher in the seminary.[13] In other words, as the scholar Sajjad Rizvi writes, "Even if the *mujtahids* decided on the *marāji'*, without popular acceptance their *marja'iyya* would be ineffective."[14] This reality is believed to be protected by the hidden influence of the Twelfth Imam, as the maraji are his representatives and so only those worthy of reaching the rank of marja are actually able to become widely followed through the Imam's divine support.

This dyad of religious authority—the marja and followers—reflects the principles of the allegiance (*bayah*) and treaties that the Prophet Mohammed practiced with Muslims and non-Muslims as a political leader. A marja proposes himself and people accept his marja'iyya and begin to follow, thus turning a potential marja into a real one.[15] This legitimation acts as the basis of an undeclared contract:

believers will establish a marja and follow his decrees in exchange for him providing guidance and certifying their religious deeds as valid.

Sistani's reclusive nature has made his marja'iyya even more opaque, partly building up mystique around him and making him the least accessible marja in history.[16] This presents a contradiction— a marja who is a recluse yet arguably the most powerful marja of all time— which is part of why Sistani's role is unprecedented. Sistani does not give speeches or grant interviews, rarely makes statements, does not publish his works, does not teach in public, and has been seen out of his home only a handful of times in the last twenty-five years. Making any meaningful direct contact with him is very rare—usually, messages are conveyed through intermediaries, which is a significant departure from the practices of his predecessors and contemporaries. This makes studying Sistani a tricky task, forcing the researcher to rely on official statements and the insights of third parties.

There is very little published source material on Sistani before 2003, so it is difficult to compare how his views changed over time. While it is reasonable to expect that he remained committed to his principles, especially those around the role of the maraji in the modern world, his post-2003 experiences probably had an effect on some of his views. The history of Iran, especially that from 1979 onwards, also presumably gave Sistani much to reflect on vis-à-vis politics and clerical authority.[17] The outcomes of key interventions Sistani undertook in Iraq, such as the push for elections and the constitution, forging consensus among Shia parties, and his 2014 decree calling for Iraqis to rise up to fight the Islamic State, also clearly led him to evaluate his stance, as we shall see. Unfortunately, however, there is little documentation on how Sistani's thinking changed. This opacity around Sistani the man and the marja is part of why the marja'iyya can be described as a closed institution.

One of the structural features of the marja'iyya that gives it strength and adds to the opacity of decision-making processes is its polycephalic nature.[18] Multiple maraji exist at the same time, and each has their own authority that they exercise in different ways. This can lead to a balancing of power among the maraji, or fragmentation. But in the case of Najaf, that usually leads to the emergence of a top tier of maraji who take on more of a political role, while the others remain limited to jurisprudence. For much of the past twenty-five years, Najaf has had four senior maraji, the ayatollahs Muhammad Saeed al-Hakim (d. 2021), Muhammad Ishaq al-Fayyadh, Bashir Hussain al-Najafi, and Sistani. Sometimes, a primus inter pares emerges, as was the case with the maraji Muhsin Hakim (d. 1970), Abu al-Qasim Khoei (d. 1992), and Sistani. But there can also be competition and opposing views. Such competition emerged during the time of Akhund Khurasani (d. 1911) and Sayed Yazdi (d. 1919) in the early twentieth century, both of whom were the senior maraji of their time.[19] Currently, the maraji in Najaf support Sistani's leadership. Further, the Najafi tradition, in which clerics advise politicians but do not rule directly, is widely supported—including in Qom, where several maraji follow the Najafi tradition.

2
Sistani the Man and Marja

In this chapter, I attempt to present a summarized political biography of Sistani, highlighting his interventions and the context behind them. Some of the information presented here is being published for the first time, and while not exhaustive, this chapter gives a clear idea of Sistani's political role in Iraq.

The Formative Years

Ali al-Hussaini al-Sistani was born in the city of Mashhad, Iran, on August 4, 1930, to a clerical family that traces its lineage to Imam Ali and Fatima al-Zahra, the daughter of the Prophet Mohammed.[1] Among his ancestors is Muhammad Baqir Astarabadi (d. 1631), more popularly known as Mir Damad, who is one of the most revered scholars in Shia Islam and a pioneer of the hawza of Isfahan. Mir Damad's great-great-grandson, Sayed Muhammad, was appointed Shaykh al-Islam of the Sistan region (modern-day eastern Iran) in the early seventeenth century by the Safavid shah Hussain I, after which the family became known by the Sistani name. Sayed Muhammad's sons gradually moved back to Isfahan, where they felt more at home, and one of his grandsons, Sayed Ibrahim, moved to Mashhad and established the Sistani family there.

Ayatollah Sistani's grandfather and namesake, Ali al-Sistani (d. 1922), was the first of the family to be born in Mashhad, though he also studied and taught in Najaf and Samarra for many years before returning to Mashhad in 1900.[2] Following the elder Ali al-Sistani's death, his son Muhammad Baqir (d. 1951) took his place as a prayer leader in Goharshad Mosque, adjacent to the Imam al-Ridha shrine.[3]

Ayatollah Sistani's mother was the daughter of Sayed Ridha al-Mahrabani al-Sarabi, a cleric in Mashhad.[4] Sistani had five younger brothers, Mahmoud, Hadi (still alive), Ibrahim, Jawad and Hussain; and seven sisters from his father's first marriage.[5]

In a visit to Mashhad in 1955, Sistani married the daughter of Sayed Hasan Ali Agha Shirazi, grandson of Mirza Shirazi. Sistani and his wife have seven children, five daughters and two sons, Muhammad Ridha (b. 1962) who manages his office and is a highly regarded scholar in his own right, and Muhammad Baqir (b. 1967) also a notable scholar in Najaf.[6]

Sistani's clerical career as a student is divided into three parts: the first in Mashhad between the ages of five and nineteen; the second in Qom between the ages of nineteen and twenty-one; and the third in Najaf between the ages of twenty-one and thirty-one. In Mashhad, he enrolled in a religious school and started learning the Quran, Arabic, and primary education. Then, in early 1941, he formally enrolled in the hawza of Mashhad studying the Islamic disciplines.

From early on in his education, Sistani's intelligence was on display. He excelled in his studies and quickly reached advanced stages in his seminary classes. He was fond of philosophy and its use in the Islamic sciences, but one of his teachers, Mirza Mahdi al-Isfahani (d. 1946), who was a fierce critic of philosophy, led him to "become neutral in the matter, neither supporting nor condemning [its study]," as quoted by Abd al-Adhim al-Muhtadi al-Bahrani.[7] By the end of 1949, Sistani had completed the highest level of courses available in Mashhad in *fiqh* (jurisprudence), *usul* (methodology and principles of jurisprudence), theology, and philosophy, and decided to relocate to Qom, where the hawza had a range of teachers with even greater depth.[8]

In Qom, Sistani attended the lectures of several senior scholars, including Ayatollah Muhammad al-Hujjah al-Kuhkamari (d. 1953) in fiqh. But Sistani was most dedicated to the classes of Ayatollah Hussain al-Tabatabaei al-Burujerdi (d. 1961), under whom he studied fiqh and usul for two years.[9] Of all the nearly thirty teachers that Sistani had through various stages, Burujerdi had the greatest impact on him, in both his religious and political ideology.[10] Burujerdi was the most senior marja in Iran and frequently coaxed the state into respecting Islamic law, using his position and network to mobilize mass support and pressure the government, without advocating for revolution or the direct rule of clerics, as other scholars called for.[11]

In addition to observing up close the centrist pragmatism of Burujerdi, during his time in Qom the young Sistani was also exposed to the different wings of the clerical movement. The revolutionary wing was represented by Ayatollah Ruhollah Khomeini, who fervently supported clerical oversight and, later, rule; and the conformist wing was allied to the shah and believed clerics should stay out of politics.[12] During the years (1949–51) that Sistani spent in Qom, tension was increasing between Khomeini and Burujerdi, with the latter issuing an injunction banning hawza students from joining parties or entering politics.[13] This was also the time when the hawza of Qom increased its prestige, growing in size, stature, and organization, and Burujerdi became the highest religious authority for Shia Muslims globally, and gained deference from the Shah. This period was formative for Sistani, and would shape his views and behavior when he became a marja and faced similar tribulations in dealing with governments and clerics.[14]

In late 1951, Sistani, then twenty-one, decided to relocate to Najaf to further his studies, residing in the Bukharaei school in the

Huwaysh quarter of the old city.[15] According to the late Sheikh Hussain al-Amini, who met Sistani upon his arrival in December 1951, Sistani was already a mujtahid when he entered Najaf.[16] During the next decade, Sistani studied Islamic sciences under several senior scholars, including Ayatollah Muhsin al-Hakim and Ayatollah Mahmud al-Shahrudi (d. 1974), but mostly under the tutelage of Ayatollah Abu al-Qasim al-Khoei (d. 1992) and Ayatollah Hussain al-Hilli (d. 1974).[17] Hilli's ascetic personality and lifestyle is the one Sistani most closely identified with and chose as a role model.[18] After mastering the Islamic sciences, Sistani prepared to return permanently to Mashhad in mid-1961. In recognition of his extraordinary talent, his teachers Khoei and Hilli each issued him with a very rare license of ijtihad.[19] His stay in Mashhad only lasted for six months, whereupon he returned to Najaf and has remained since.[20]

His return in early 1962 marked the beginning of the next phase of his clerical career, now as a teacher of the *bahth al-kharij* stage in the hawza (the most advanced course of study), which lasted until August 1992 with the death of Khoei. (At that point, Sistani became a marja.)[21] Sistani first taught fiqh, and then began teaching usul in late 1964. By the early 1970s, he had risen to prominence as one of the next generation of elite mujtahids and among the top students of Khoei, who had become the supreme marja of the Shia, but remained dedicated to teaching and managed to avoid the fame of some of his peers like Ayatollah Muhammad Baqir al-Sadr.[22] Sistani was part of Khoei's prestigious *istifta* (issuing rulings) committee in the 1960s and 1970s; the committee answered religious queries based on Khoei's jurisprudential views.[23] In the early 1980s, Sistani expanded his classes to include lectures on *hadith* and *rijal* (sciences of verifying content and transmitters of narrations from the Prophet and Imams), but he was still mostly unknown beyond a select elite in the hawza.[24] During this stage of his career, Sistani wrote more than forty works, the vast majority of which remain in unpublished manuscript form.[25] There are over fifteen published works based on his classes written by his students.[26]

The 1970s and 1980s were a troubled period for the Najaf hawza, with scholars being imprisoned, deported, and executed, as Saddam Hussein's regime attempted to control the hawza through fear and manipulation.[27] With the execution of Sadr in April 1980, the government showed that no one was untouchable.[28] Sistani was almost deported during the Iran–Iraq War, but despite the severe pressure the hawza was under, he managed to continue with his career in Najaf. This period was also formative for Sistani as he observed up close how Khoei reacted to the unprecedented attacks on the hawza, how he dealt with the internal pressures and demands to react, and the upheavals in Iraq as a result of the Islamic revolution in Iran.

In early 1986, the circle that made up the office and entourage of Khoei began to petition him to prepare a successor, following the sudden death in December 1985 of Sayed Nasr Allah al-Tabrizi, known as al-Mustanbit, who was touted as a future marja and was Khoei's son-in-law.[29] There were at least ten qualified mujtahids in Najaf from Khoei's school who had all established themselves as a potential marja and had published works underlying their credentials and well-attended classes, putting them ahead of Sistani, at least from the perspective of the social hierarchy of the hawza.[30] But perhaps because of Sistani's humility and wish to avoid the limelight, in addition to his scholarly skill, Khoei and some of his close advisors instead began to call on Sistani to assume more responsibility.[31] In early December 1988, Khoei fell ill and, upon visiting him, Sistani was essentially ordered by Khoei to assume his position as prayer leader in the Khadhra Mosque adjacent to the Imam Ali Shrine, where Khoei had taught and led prayers for many decades.[32] On December 16, 1988 Sistani began leading the prayers in the Khadhra Mosque, which he would continue until June 10, 1994, when the mosque was permanently closed by Saddam's regime. This move by

Khoei had the desired effect in terms of raising Sistani's profile, and he became known to larger numbers of clerics and laypeople, who also began to accept him as Khoei's chosen and natural successor.[33]

The 1990 Gulf War put the marja'iyya into near conflict with the state, especially following the beginning of the uprising in Najaf on March 3, 1991.[34] As rebels overran regime forces, they looked to senior clerics for leadership and to give them greater momentum. On March 7, Khoei issued a statement, naming a committee of nine scholars to oversee general affairs in the absence of the state, to provide stability and guidance. This move was understood by supporters and opponents as backing the uprising (which later became known as the Intifadha). A week later, regime forces turned the tide and began to encircle Najaf, deploying heavy weaponry and helicopters, as the U.S.-led coalition declined to intervene, despite the fact that President George H. W. Bush had encouraged the uprising. By March 20, regime forces had reached the old city in Najaf, then proceeded to arrest Ayatollah Khoei and took him under duress to meet Saddam in a televised meeting, in an effort to quell the remaining rebels.[35] The Intifadha was brutally crushed and the thousands of summary executions and forced disappearances extended to clerics in Najaf.[36]

By now, the regime was well aware of Sistani's position, and on March 25, 1991, in the aftermath of the Intifadha, he and his sons were detained by the regime—along with other senior maraji, such as Ayatollah Murtadha al-Burujerdi, Ayatollah Mirza Ali al-Gharawi, and more than a hundred other prominent mujtahids and scholars. Sistani and a group of seventeen clerics were first taken to the Salam Hotel in Najaf, which was requisitioned by regime forces, for interrogation, and then to al-Razazah military camp near Karbala, and finally to al-Radhwaniya detention facility on the outskirts of Baghdad. During his detention, the interrogators asked Sistani to sign a statement denouncing the Intifadha and blaming Iran for fomenting violence against the state. After Sistani's refusal, he was beaten and tortured before being released back to Najaf a week later.[37]

The crushing of the Intifadha had disastrous effects on Najaf, with scholars detained and executed, schools and libraries looted, destroyed, and shut down, and a state of terror imposed on the city for several months. The regime had found an opportunity to purge the hawza once again and weaken the marja'iyya, using its network of spies to identify targets. On August 8, 1992, Khoei passed away at his home in Kufa, with the regime immediately shutting down power, communications, and roads in Najaf to prevent crowds gathering. A select group was allowed to take part in the funeral and burial of Khoei, with Sistani leading the prayers.[38] The next day, a mourning service was held at the Khadhra Mosque, with Saddam's envoy Rokan al-Majid attending and giving his condolences to Sistani.[39] These events marked the next stage of Sistani's life—that of a marja—which would bring with it great responsibility and much danger.[40]

The Early Marja'iyya

Immediately upon Khoei's passing, Sistani began to be referred to as a marja by senior figures in Najaf, such as Ayatollah Ali al-Beheshti (Khoei's closest friend) and Burujerdi. Khoei's office, led by his son Muhammad Taqi, referred religious queries to Sistani, so that more people became aware of what the preferred succession was. Sistani reluctantly accepted his new role and began writing his book on Islamic law, completing it in September 1992.[41] He also took up Khoei's teaching seat in the Khadhra Mosque, but it would still be some time yet before he gained recognition beyond Najaf. Several notable students of Khoei and Sistani, as well as other senior clerics in the hawzas of Najaf and Qom and beyond, known as *ahl al-khibra*, or people of expertise, backed his marja'iyya and testified that he was the most knowledgeable of the maraji.[42] As Sistani's marja'iyya grew by gradual consolidation, it coexisted with more than twenty others in the Shia world. It was important to its success that it could attract followers abroad, at a time when the Iraqi regime was so oppressive and limited Sistani domestically.[43]

Two factors helped establish Sistani's marja'iyya and expand it into other countries. First were the efforts of his son-in-law and representative, Sayed Jawad al-Shahrestani, based in Qom. Shahrestani opened offices on Sistani's behalf in the Middle East and eventually the rest of the world, published Sistani's works on Islamic sciences, organized the network of representatives, collected religious taxes and managed charitable distributions, and began paying the stipends of students in the hawzas of Iran, Syria, Lebanon, and elsewhere. These efforts brought international recognition to Sistani's status as a marja and began the process of reaching the position of supreme marja. As Sistani himself was virtually out of reach and Saddam retained an iron grip on Iraq, Shahrestani was the marja by proxy, and his charismatic nature and resources made it possible for Sistani's marja'iyya to reach more people than other marja'iyyas could reach.

The second important factor in establishing Sistani's marja'iyya was the death of other senior maraji from Khoei's generation soon after his passing. This ensured Sistani faced little competition from more senior scholars. Most of Khoei's millions of followers among the laypeople turned to Sistani, giving him an advantage.[44] In Najaf, his position became uncontested after the death of Ayatollah Abd al-Alaa al-Sabzawari in August 1993. Sabzawari was Sistani's senior by twenty years and was a classmate of Khoei; his marja'iyya was widely recognized, but he died earlier than expected. In Qom, the deaths of Ayatollahs Muhammad Ridha al-Gulpaygani (d. December 1993), Muhammad Ali al-Araki (d. November 1994), and Muhammad al-Rouhani (d. August 1997) ensured that most of their followers reverted to Sistani, giving him the largest following among the remaining maraji.[45] This gave Sistani the position of senior marja among the Shia Muslims. He was not yet the undisputed supreme marja (that would happen after 2003), but he was on the path to that status.

This position did not grant Sistani immunity from the Saddam regime, however. First, in June 1994, the regime closed the Khadhra Mosque where Sistani taught and led prayers. Second, in November 1996, he survived an assassination attempt at his home, during which one of his staff was killed. Third, in April 1997, an assassination attempt on his financial secretary in Kashif Al-Ghita Mosque almost succeeded. After a group of his students were deported in early 1998, Sistani stopped teaching openly, closed his office and home to the public, and decided to remain indoors for the next few years, not leaving his home at all, as a form of protest. This reclusion signaled his opposition to the regime, but without giving it a means to attack him.[46]

However, the government was still able to attack the hawza. It assassinated Burujerdi in April 1998, Gharawi in June 1998, and Sadr in February 1999. The security and intelligence services maintained a constant presence outside Sistani's home and surveilled him and his key staff and advisors, causing much hardship for the Sistani family and for his supporters and followers.[47]

The ten-year period between 1992 and 2002 was the most challenging in Sistani's life, having lost his mentor and several close colleagues, with the regime imposing suffocating control over Najaf.[48] His freedom was severely limited, and the danger to himself and his family was ever present.[49] Communications with the outside world were monitored by the regime, forcing reliance on messages smuggled with pilgrims.

Sistani had inherited the marja'iyya in unenviable circumstances and during a difficult time, during which he could not exercise much of the duties and privileges of the position, such as teaching, welcoming influential delegations, overseeing religious, scholarly, and charitable projects, and extending guidance to Shia communities across the globe. Iraqis also suffered under the strain of sanctions and the future looked very bleak for the hawza, in particular.[50] The number of students and teachers in Najaf had dropped from more than 15,000 in the 1960s and 1970s to less than 1,000 in the 1990s.[51] In February 2004, Sistani's son, Muhammad Ridha, described this difficult period, saying that the hawza of Najaf "has suffered severe calamities in recent decades, and as a result it has lost many of its prominent scholars, writers, and thinkers, who were killed, imprisoned, exiled, and displaced, and only a few of those distinguished people remain."[52] Sistani felt great responsibility for protecting the thousand-year-old Najaf hawza and the status of the marja'iyya, but had little means to do so apart from avoiding antagonizing the regime.[53] While Sistani's marja'iyya enjoyed much better conditions outside Iraq, he and those close to him lived a life effectively under siege.

This period also witnessed competing dynamics, internally and externally, around the marja'iyya. Saddam's regime had been trying for years to gain control over the hawza and to create a loyal class of clerics, through such measures as infiltrating the hawza, deporting clerics, closing schools, and general manipulation.[54] This even extended to trying to promote a state-sponsored "Arab marja'iyya."[55] In June 2003, Sistani's office (likely written by Muhammad Ridha) issued a statement that said, "the previous regime sought to make the hawza an Arab one and the marja'iyya an Iraqi one, but it failed to achieve that."[56] The regime's efforts did cause strife in Najaf, and while it ultimately failed to achieve its goals, it did foster suspicions among the clerical elite as to who was in contact with the regime or benefiting from state support.

In 1994 in Najaf, Ayatollah Muhammad al-Sadr had used his marja'iyya to create a religious movement that took advantage of the regime's relaxations on religiosity (called the Faith Campaign by Saddam on its launch in June 1993). Utilizing the regime's new stance on Islam, Sadr was able to inspire a generation of young Shia Iraqis, who later evolved into the Sadrist trend.[57] (Today's Sadrist movement is associated with Muqtada al-Sadr, who took over leadership of his father's movement.) Ayatollah Sadr was able to gain control of some aspects of the hawza, such as administration of schools, residency permits for non-Iraqi seminarians, exemptions from military service for Iraqi students, and prayer services in mosques and shrines.[58] This led to criticism in Najaf and abroad as to what Sadr's intentions were and whether he was in league with the regime and had become the state-sponsored marja they were seeking.[59] Sadr's claim that he was the most knowledgeable marja of all time, and later that he was the leader of all Muslims, offended other maraji and the Iranian regime, which put Sadr under even more suspicion.

The criticism stung Sadr: he viewed himself as reviving the power of the Iraqi Shia, while the traditional hawza was subdued.[60] This led him to coin the term "the vocal hawza" (al-hawza al-natiqa) to describe the hawza he controlled in opposition to "the silent hawza," which was a derogatory reference to Sistani and the other maraji.[61] Sadr himself noted the cold reception he received from Sistani in one of their meetings, as a response to the former's increased power in Najaf.[62] The discord between the Sistani and Sadr marja'iyya and their partisans continued even after Sadr's assassination in 1999, peaking in 2003 and 2004. It has since dissipated, and the two camps have even become somewhat cooperative since 2016.

In Beirut, Muhammad Hussain Fadhlallah (d. 2010), who had been Khoei's and briefly Sistani's representative—and who had acknowledged Sistani being the most knowledgeable marja—launched his own marja'iyya in April 1995, which led to many Lebanese Shia and others in Western countries to follow him.[63] Meanwhile, in Tehran, Ali Khamenei began his marja'iyya in December 1994, combining his political role as supreme leader of the Islamic Republic of Iran (an office he assumed in 1989) with that of religious authority in the traditional role of marja. Khamenei's was and still is the biggest challenge to Sistani's marja'iyya, due to the resources and formal political power of Khamenei's marja'iyya, which provides an alternate model of religious leadership and authority.

As noted above, Sistani had adopted a reclusive attitude to overcome these challenges, and a policy of non-antagonism to detractors,

competitors and the state. Such a posture may appear to be antitheti-
cal to leadership—yet he retained popularity throughout this period.
In the lead-up to the invasion of Iraq, the government even sought
to use Sistani's position to garner support and build up a resistance
movement. In September 2002, state television broadcast a "fatwa"
ascribed to Sistani: "The duty of Muslims in these difficult circumstances is to unite . . . and do all they can to defend beloved Iraq and
safeguard it against the schemes of the covetous enemies. . . . Every
Muslim should do all he can to defend Muslim Iraq and prevent the
aggression against it. . . . Offering any kind of assistance or help to
the aggressors is a mortal sin."[64] A similar ruling ascribed to Sistani
was broadcast in March 2003 as the invasion began, but in both
cases the rulings have not been verified by Sistani's office, and were
likely pure state propaganda.[65]

This incident shows the contradictory nature of the state's relationship with Sistani, trying to weaken and control him at the same
time that it promoted his position and sought legitimacy from him.

Establishing the New Iraq

Following the invasion of Iraq and regime change in April 2003, the
importance of Sistani's position became clearer to the international
community, which had not expected him to have a prominent role
in the new Iraq.[66] But the security situation in Najaf was particularly fraught and remained so for some time, leading to armed
gangs, described as Sadrists, congregating near Sistani's house and
threatening him.[67] His office noted, a week after regime change,
that Sistani's life was still in danger: "After the fall of the regime,
there was a security breakdown in the holy city of Najaf, and armed
groups of evil and corrupt people appeared, and unfortunate incidents took place, and security is still not guaranteed in the city, and
there are risks that threaten the lives of the maraji, especially His
Eminence."[68] Sistani did not believe that regime change by invasion

was the best approach: "It was not desired to change the tyranni-cal regime through invasion and occupation, with the many trage-dies that entailed, including the collapse of the foundations of the Iraqi state, insecurity and stability, exacerbation of crimes, and the destruction of much public property by burning, looting, damage, and so on," his office stated in February 2004.[69]

Immediately following the collapse of Saddam's regime in April 2003, chaos reigned. Khoei's son, Sayed Abd al-Majid, was killed on his return from exile. Government offices and public property were looted. Acts of revenge and general disorder, in Najaf and across Iraq, caused the Shia population to turn to Sistani for leadership. In response, Sistani's office released several statements condemning the looting and violence and placing responsibility on Coalition forces for maintaining security and order.[70]

Sistani viewed the U.S.-led Coalition as an occupying force, and he did not criticize those who resisted them. He also did not call on people to cooperate with the occupying forces, as he was "very concerned about their goals."[71] In his view, the best way to end the occupation was for Iraqi sovereignty to be restored, which would naturally lead to the departure of foreign forces. Armed confron-tation with the occupation was not suitable at the time, but if the occupying powers would not hand over sovereignty to Iraq, then Sistani indicated that his view could change.

On April 20, 2003, Sistani's office issued answers to religious queries on the status of public property, weapons of the security forces, and Sunni mosques. These statements are an early record of Sistani's attempts to uphold the rule of law, protect the institutions of the state, and prevent sectarian strife.[72] This marked the beginning of a transformation in Najaf's previous approach to the state, from one based on distrust of the state because of how it treated the Shia to a more involved statesmanship. One of these answers was telling and seemingly addressed to both clerics in Iraq and the exiles looking to take up positions in the new Iraq: "It is not right to involve the clergy in the administrative aspects." The aim was to keep clerics away from direct involvement in government and politics, in contrast to the Iranian system, and protect the hawza from the inevitable criticisms that politicians face. While many clerics adhered to his warning, others in established and new political parties ignored it.[73]

Both the Iraqi opposition who had returned to take eventual control of Iraq and the U.S.-led Coalition had underestimated Sistani's willingness to speak out on political matters, and had expected his role to be similar to what it was prior to regime change. When it began to be clear to them that Sistani was going to be influential on the political process and that Shia Iraqis would look to him for leadership, the Coalition attempted to organize meetings with Sistani to understand his positions and policies.

But Sistani's approach to meetings was to limit them to high-level politicians, clerics, and international figures. He refused to meet with American officials and those who represented the occupying Coalition administration and forces. Over time, having discovered they were not fully prepared to heed his guidance, he limited his interaction with Iraqi politicians as he did not want them to take advantage of the propaganda value or convey a sense of approval from Sistani. He allowed visits from UN representatives and religious figures inside Iraq and from the region. According to one American journalist who was based in Iraq for several years from 2003, Sistani's meetings with religious and ethnic community leaders between 2003 and 2009 showed "a deep commitment to pluralism, an effort to prevent sectarianism [from] completely consuming the country, and an urging to respect minorities."[74]

Regime change had dramatically changed Sistani's role and gave him the opportunity to develop a platform to expand his religious authority into the political realm.[75] As the opinion of Sistani in the new Iraq became prominent, the foreign press began to address questions to his office to understand his position on the coalition presence and his own vision for politics.[76] In May and June 2003,

Sistani's office in Najaf, overseen by Muhammad Ridha, gave two telling responses. The first was on the role of the marja'iyya in the new state: "The marja'iyya does not exercise a role in (state) authority and governance." The second concerned the role a marja plays in life in general: "The main role of the marja is to provide the believers with religious fatwas in various matters of individual and social life, but there are other tasks that the marja performs by virtue of his social and religious status, including helping the poor and taking care of religious institutions and centers and so on."[77]

Then came the explicit response on whether Sistani adhered to the Iranian model of wilayat al-faqih in Iraq. The answer was simple: "The formation of a religious government on the basis of the idea of absolute wilayat al-faqih is not feasible."[78]

Sistani's office then weighed in on the role of clerics in government: "The marja'iyya is of the opinion that religious scholars distance themselves from assuming government positions."[79]

Finally, the office issued a statement about whether Sistani supported establishing a religious government in Iraq: "The main political and social forces in Iraq do not call for the establishment of a religious government, but rather for the establishment of a system that respects the religious fundamentals of Iraqis and adopts the principles of pluralism, justice, and equality."[80]

These statements made it clear, to Sistani's Shia audience and politicians as well as foreigners, that he did not wish for a theocracy to be established in Iraq. The question, then, became about what kind of state he did want, and how such a state would be established.

In April 2003, in the aftermath of the collapse of the Iraqi state, Sistani made it clear that he would not support the imposition of foreign rule: "Governance in Iraq should be for the Iraqis without any foreign domination, and the Iraqis are the ones who have the right to choose the type of regime in Iraq without the interference of foreigners." As soon as the Coalition Provisional Authority (CPA) was established, with Paul Bremer ruling by decree, and it became clear that the United States envisaged a slow handover to a handpicked government, Sistani began a campaign to force the United States into a new direction.

First, in June 2003, Sistani stated: "The shape of the new Iraq is determined by the Iraqi people with all their ethnicities and sects, and the mechanism for this is free and direct elections."[81] Throughout the summer a version of this statement was repeated: "The form of governance in Iraq is determined by the Iraqi people, and the mechanism for this is to hold general elections so that every Iraqi chooses someone to represent them in a constituent assembly to write the constitution, and then the constitution approved by this council is put to the people for a vote."[82]

When the CPA announced that it would form a council to write the new Iraqi constitution, disregarding Sistani's call that the Iraqi people elect an assembly to draft the constitution, Sistani responded with a decree. The fatwa, stamped with his personal seal, was issued on June 25, 2003, and rejected the CPA move:

> Those authorities do not have any right to appoint members of the constitution drafting council, nor is there a guarantee that this council will draft a constitution that matches the higher interests of the Iraqi people and expresses its national identity, whose foundations are the pure Islamic religion and noble social values, so the aforementioned project is fundamentally unacceptable, and first general elections must be held in order for every Iraqi eligible to vote to choose someone to represent them in a constituent assembly to write the constitution, and then a general vote will take place on the constitution approved by this council.[83]

The fatwa was Sistani's first political intervention as a marja, and it was significantly based on the democratic principles of the right to representation and self-determination.[84] It signaled the new marja'iyya that Sistani headed, one that would play a different role in politics from its earlier form and that of previous maraji.

The CPA, led by Bremer, had underestimated the strength of Sistani's opposition and his influence.[85] The assassination of Ayatollah Muhammad Baqir al-Hakim in an August 2003 bomb attack in Najaf left Sistani as the sole clerical authority on political matters in Iraq.[86] Whatever plans the United States had for Iraq were suddenly challenged by the handwritten notes of an elderly cleric in Najaf. The fatwa about the drafting of the constitution forced the CPA to change its approach, holding caucuses to appoint a transitional assembly that would then select an interim government. However, this approach was still not in line with the direct national elections that Sistani was calling for. The CPA announced its plan on November 15, 2003; Sistani pushed back on November 27, 2003:

> His Eminence has some reservations about the aforementioned plan. First, it is based on the preparation of the Iraqi state law for the transitional period by the Governing Council in agreement with the occupying power, and this does not confer on it the status of legitimacy, but to become so it must be presented to the representatives of the Iraqi people for approval. Second, the mechanism contained in it for electing members of the Transitional Legislative Council does not guarantee the formation of a council that truly represents the Iraqi people, so it must be replaced by another mechanism that guarantees this, which is the elections, so that the council emanates from the will of the Iraqis and represents them fairly, and is free from any challenge to its legitimacy.[87]

For the next two months, Bremer attempted to push through Sistani's opposition, initially by insisting on his road map and then as a concession by stating that the CPA would hand over limited sovereignty to an interim government in June 2004 and that there would not be enough time for elections before then. Sistani responded indirectly through representatives in Baghdad and Basra, who began a series of demonstrations, attended by hundreds of thousands, calling for elections as soon as possible.[88] This mass mobilization served as notice of Sistani's power, and from that moment onward it became clear to all that avoiding conflict with him would be a necessity in Iraqi politics. A delegation from the CPA-appointed Governing Council visited Sistani on January 22, 2004, to inform him that elections would not be held in 2004, which Sistani feared meant an interim government chosen by the United States would remain in power indefinitely. Eventually, negotiations led to an agreement that elections would be held in January 2005, but Sistani would still not give any legitimacy to the interim government formed in June 2004.[89] His position on a government chosen by Iraqis was consistent: "What we want is to allow the formation of a government emanating from the will of the Iraqi people with all their sects and ethnicities" and "Iraqis of all sects and confessions, Shia and others, are united in demanding respect for their will in determining their own destiny and refusing to allow foreigners to plan their political, economic, social, or cultural future."[90]

Sistani's concerns were principally related to government and legislation enacted by a foreign power that did not reflect the will or input of the people, therefore lacking legitimacy and undermining the sovereignty of Iraq. His opposition to the CPA appointing an interim government and drafting a constitution under its supervision was based on concern that the United States would seek to impose a government on Iraq rather than allow one to be devised organically. Thus, Sistani made his criticism clear, early on, of the CPA approach of using the Governing Council to draft a constitution: "It is necessary . . . for the next constitution to be written based on [elections] . . . there is no legitimacy for any constitution written by appointed persons, whether by the occupying power or members of the so-called Governing Council or others."[91]

Sistani's fears were realized with the passing of the Transitional Administrative Law (TAL) in March 2004, which acted as an interim constitution, drafted by American officials and approved by hand-picked members of the Governing Council.[92] Sistani feared the TAL would enshrine political precedents and principles and establish articles that would be difficult to reverse later. Lakhdar Brahimi, the UN special envoy to Iraq, asked Sistani for his view on the TAL. Sistani replied with a long and detailed criticism of the TAL, the CPA approach, and the enshrinement of sectarianism in politics.[93]

Upon being informed that the United States had introduced wording to the draft of UN Security Council Resolution 1546 that gave legitimacy to the TAL, Sistani wrote a letter to the UN Security Council warning them of the grave repercussions of this inclusion. The final resolution removed the reference to the TAL.[94] This incident demonstrated Sistani's willingness to escalate his opposition to U.S. attempts to rule Iraq by proxy, and the seriousness with which he viewed his authority and the opinions of the marja'iyya in general: they were not to be ignored or circumvented, even by a superpower. It also showed the importance Sistani attached to the UN role in Iraq, which he understood to have more legitimacy than the United States. Sistani's interactions with the UN since 2003 have been consistently cooperative.[95] Sistani and the UN have remained completely aligned on their political stances, starting with the right to self-rule.[96]

Despite Sistani's repeated opposition to empowering unelected officials, the interim government to which the CPA handed over partial power in June 2004 became a political reality. Even as Sistani underlined that this interim government lacked legitimacy, he still gave guidance to it.[97] This pragmatism has been at the core of his approach to dealing with subsequent governments—giving guidance without conferring any of his own political capital or authority.[98]

Dealing with Muqtada al-Sadr

Among the most challenging days of the 2003–4 period for Sistani were those involving Muqtada al-Sadr, who did not recognize Sistani's authority. Sadr violently clashed with coalition forces, denounced CPA-installed Iraqi politicians, and sought to gain control of shrines and religious institutions.

Sistani intervened in several incidents involving Sadr. One was in Karbala in October 2003, after Sadrists moved to take control of the Imam Hussain Shrine, leading to clashes with police and Coalition forces. Sistani led a mediation between the conflicting parties, which yielded a settlement and withdrawal of the Sadrists.[99]

In another instance, in April 2004, the Sadrists took control of the Imam Ali Shrine in Najaf, setting up a sharia court and offices for their movement. In the meantime, they continued clashing with U.S. forces in Najaf and Baghdad. Sistani's office was not able to broker a compromise and the CPA appointed a new governor for Najaf, specifically for the task of reigning in Muqtada Al-Sadr.[100] The CPA attitude toward Sadr hardened when the body accused him of being connected to the murder of Abd al-Majid al-Khoei in April 2003, and attempted to arrest him.[101] Meanwhile, Sadr's control of Najaf's old city led to severe tensions with the hawza, with several violent incidents happening, including around Sistani's home. These clashes led to some members of the hawza issuing a letter criticizing Sadr's movement.[102] On May 19, 2004, Sistani called for all armed forces to withdraw from Najaf, but neither Sadr nor the United States heeded his call.[103]

Going into the summer of 2004, the situation in Najaf deteriorated, leading to a full-scale battle between Sadr's Mahdi Army and American forces on August 5, 2004. That same day, Sistani was moved to Baghdad and eventually arrived in London for medical treatment.[104] For the next three weeks, the conflict escalated and was largely fought around the Imam Ali Shrine, ending only when Sistani returned to Najaf and brokered a ceasefire on August 27.[105] Sistani undertook a risky journey from Basra to Najaf while a battle was still taking place in the old city, with tens of thousands joining him as part of a convoy, a historic moment of a marja physically leading the masses, something not seen for decades.

Critics of Sistani believe his departure from Najaf was coordinated to give cover to the Coalition military effort to remove Sadr from the shrine, and when that effort broke down Sistani returned to force a resolution.[106] Whatever the background to the events of August 2004, Sistani did manage to prevent further violence, got Sadr to accept a withdrawal, took back control of the shrine, and kept U.S. forces away from the old city, using only the power of his popular authority.[107] If there had been any doubt, now it was clear that Sistani was the most powerful figure in Iraq.

Sadr's attempt to present an alternative clerical authority to Sistani's was rejected by the rest of the hawza in Najaf.[108] However, it provided continuity for his father's followers, and Sadr's relations with Ayatollah Kadhim al-Haeri in Qom—who provided legal cover for Sadr—posed a challenge to Sistani's leadership. The Iranian regime supported Sadr as a means to weaken American control in Iraq, while knowing that support for Sadr would be seen in Najaf as an attempt to undermine Sistani. In response, Sistani began to gradually exert more control over the shrines and institutionalize his marja'iyya. As Sadr clashed with the government and other political parties in the coming years, it was Sistani who often protected him at times of crisis, thereby steadily reinforcing Sistani's authority in Najaf.

Formation of the State, 2005–6

The period 2003–5 witnessed much instability where rule of law was absent at several points, the state had limited sovereignty, and the institutions of government were weak. During this time, people were still adjusting to the post-Saddam period, and some questioned what the status of public property, finances, and even territory were given the U.S.-led occupation. Sistani responded to several religious queries related to such topics, in which he sought to reinforce the necessity of rule of law, protect Iraq's resources and integrity, and prohibit acts damaging to the public wealth.[109]

After maintaining pressure for elections to be held as soon as possible—despite some politicians arguing for their postponement—Sistani got his wish when the Independent High Electoral Commission confirmed that elections to the transitional National Assembly would be held on January 30, 2005. The National Assembly would be responsible for appointing a transitional government and drafting the constitution, which would be the first time the Iraqi state exercised sovereignty after regime change. At this point, Sistani gave the political process legitimacy, issuing a fatwa obligating citizens to register to vote (and by extension to vote): "It is obligatory for citizens eligible to vote, both male and female, to verify that their names are correctly entered in the voter register. . . . So that everyone can participate in the elections."[110] This fatwa is significant, as it was the first time Shia clerical authority was used to back democratic elections in Iraq, making participation a religious duty for the Shia.

Despite Sistani being the marja most followed by the Shia, and his position of authority in the post-2003 political order, the majority of the Shia Islamist parties did not view him as their spiritual leader and only grudgingly heeded his instructions—but still turned to him as a mediator and broker for political agreements. Shia politicians could not risk alienating Sistani or clashing with him, as they would lose, but they could benefit from his legitimacy among the Shia by aligning themselves with him. The most powerful Shia parties were the Supreme Council for Islamic Revolution in Iraq (SCIRI), the Dawa Party, and the Sadrists, followed by a broad category of other smaller parties.[111] To ensure the Shia parties did not enter into a power struggle and to keep the Sadrists in the political process, Sistani backed the formation of the United Iraqi Alliance

(UIA), which included some Sunni and minority parties, to compete in the January 2005 elections.[112] While he was careful not to give explicit backing to the Alliance, it did offer him an avenue to ensure some of his supporters were elected to the National Assembly and therefore would become part of the constitution drafting committee.[113] In essence, Sistani was seeking a way in which he could informally organize and endorse the UIA, so that Shia primacy in the elections would be guaranteed, without taking responsibility for the UIA and its subsequent performance.[114]

Thus, both the UIA and the clerical network close to Sistani began to encourage people to vote for list 169 (the UIA) as it had the "blessing" of Sistani.[115] The UIA won 140 seats in the election, and then had one of its leaders, Ibrahim al-Jaafari, elected as prime minister. The creation of the UIA was criticized by other parties, including the prime minister at the time, Ayad Allawi. Sistani's implicit backing to Shia Islamist parties, though short-lived, is still a sore point for some, including those in Najaf.[116]

During the next few months, Sistani was occupied with advising on and reviewing proposed articles of the constitution.[117] He was focused on, in the words of Mohammad R. Kalantari, "preventing the ratification of 'anti-Sharia laws' in the new Iraqi constitution."[118] In addition to having Sistani's representative Ahmad al-Safi on the constitution drafting committee, Sistani's office began to create support for the passing of the draft constitution after it was completed on September 22, 2005. It gave this support without issuing a statement or fatwa in Sistani's name.[119] Sheikh Abdul-Mahdi al-Karbalai, Sistani's representative in Karbala, delivered Sistani's urging to Iraqis to vote for the constitution in Friday prayers on October 14, 2005, despite some of the reservations the ayatollah held on specific articles.[120]

The constitution was approved by referendum on October 15, 2005, and parliamentary elections were scheduled for December 15, 2005. The poor performance of the transitional government and the parties in the UIA led Sistani to reduce his interaction with them.[121]

Still, he again issued a fatwa, on December 10, 2005, stressing the importance of voting in the elections: "These elections are no less important than the previous ones, and citizens—men and women— must participate in them [widely], in order to ensure a large and strong presence of those who are entrusted with their principles and keen on their higher interests in the next parliament. For this purpose, it is also necessary to avoid dispersing votes and expos- ing them to loss."[122] The UIA seized on the final part of the fatwa to claim that Sistani supported voting for a large alliance and, by extension the UIA, which had the greater representation of the Shia in politics.[123] Sistani's final role in this election period was to support the replacement of Jaafari with a new prime minister.[124]

Sectarian Strife

Sistani supported replacing Jaafari because Iraq had entered a bloody period of sectarian violence following the bombing of the Askari Shrine in Samarra on February 22, 2006.[125] The Iraqi government seemed incapable of imposing rule of law and preventing daily sec- tarian attacks. Sistani met with Jaafari's replacement, Nouri al-Maliki, at the end of April 2006, as he was finalizing his cabinet. Sistani gave Maliki several pieces of advice on what government priorities should be.[126] During Maliki's second visit to Sistani, in early Septem- ber 2006, Sistani adopted a more critical tone and highlighted where the government was failing.[127] Sectarian violence peaked in summer 2006, leading to Sistani releasing an open letter in his name plead- ing for an end to the killings and retributions.[128] He continued to push for Iraq regaining its full sovereignty, through the withdrawal of foreign troops, and for Iraq's politicians to take responsibility for building up the state away from sectarian interests.[129]

The year 2006 was especially violent and unstable in Iraq, and Sistani's interventions seemed to have limited effect in improving the situation. They were so ineffective, in fact, that some observers

felt that his influence was in decline.[130] Shia communities throughout Iraq, including armed groups, petitioned Sistani to issue a fatwa
obligating jihad against al-Qaeda and to defend the shrines. But
Sistani resisted, and simply denounced sectarian retribution. His
stance helped prevent a larger-scale civil war, but the immense sectarian bloodshed that had taken place so appalled and disappointed
Sistani that he had begun to reassess his political interactions and
communications.

Sistani had little success in his attempts to impress upon political leaders the necessity of improving governance and abandoning
narrow party and sectarian interests. Part of the reason for this lack
of success, however, was the influence of Iran and the United States
in electoral politics between 2003 and 2006. Sistani was competing
with these major powers, who had long-standing relations with all
of the exiled Iraqi politicians who had returned to rule—many of
whom were happy to engage in sectarian politics.

By now, Sistani was recognized across the world as the supreme
marja of the Shia, and the most important figure in Iraq. His views
and support were sought from across the region. For example, in
response to a request from the Lebanese speaker of parliament,
Nabih Berri, to help end the war with Israel in July 2006, Sistani
discreetly pushed U.S. president George W. Bush to back a ceasefire.[131]

Sistani's rise to prominence and his role in Iraq led to a backlash
internally and externally. King Abdullah of Jordan had warned in
2004 of a rising Shia crescent, and said that Sistani's "allegiance at
the end of the day will be to Iran."[132] Several messianic and sectarian movements waged a propaganda battle against him, seeking to
undermine his authority.[133] In January 2007, Iraqi and US military
forces foiled an attempt by a Shia messianic cult to assassinate Sistani.[134] In May 2007, an Al Jazeera host made comments skeptical
of Sistani's credentials and motives, which led to protests in support
of Sistani.[135] In a December 2009 Friday prayer speech, Muhammad al-Arifi, an extremist Sunni preacher in Saudi Arabia, attacked

Sistani as an infidel.[136] Several other incidents during these years and after showed that there was unease around the Middle East that Sistani had become so influential.

In 2007–8, Sistani reduced his direct interaction with politicians, while continuing to provide critical feedback through intermediaries, as he evaluated the performance of the Shia Islamist parties in particular. He had noted that the parties were trying both to associate themselves with him for the sake of propaganda, and to shift responsibility for Iraq's failings to the religious authority. In a rare audience with journalists in Najaf on September 15, 2009, Sistani stated: "In my meetings with the political parties, I tell them not to make the religious authority a front for your work. Rather, you were elected by the people so that you can assume responsibility, and you are the ones who run the country. [In] most of my meetings with politicians, I advise them not to turn my meeting into electoral propaganda for them, as they took on the responsibility and they must bear it."[137]

In fact, Sistani ended up withholding support for any of the Shia Islamist parties ahead of the January 2009 provincial elections. He expressed neutrality, while strongly encouraging voters to take part.[138]

By 2009, Sistani had become bitterly disappointed with Iraq's political elite, not least the Shia parties who claimed to be Islamists acting on his guidance. But he still believed elections were the best way to push through changes and reforms.[139] His vision for the political system, expressed back in 2004, was that one party or bloc would win elections and form a government while the other would form the opposition, and they would compete for votes through their policies and programs.[140] In this regard, Sistani did not advocate for a sectarian majority; rather, he advocated for a majoritarian government in which the winning party or bloc would be made up of different sects and ethnicities and thus be properly representative. In May 2009, ahead of national elections that were coming up in 2010, he made this view explicit once again, hoping that Iraq's political parties would change the way they contested elections and formed governments.[141] Sistani also advocated for more progressive, open lists in the election law.[142]

Over the years 2003–9, Sistani had issued numerous letters and statements to the UN, the international community, religious leaders, and even foreign leaders such as Egyptian president Hosni Mubarak, in which he expressed his opinions on current events, delivered advice, called for support for Iraq, and advocated unity among Muslims, including on the issue of Palestine.[143] He also received foreign delegations, expanded the network of social and religious establishments and activities under his supervision, and increased the reach of the marja'iyya. In this regard, he had become the supreme marja, and his opinions and interventions were deemed vital to Iraq's political order and to Shia Muslims in general. Sistani had helped the new Iraqi state take shape without giving himself a formal role, advocating for parliamentary democracy rather than religious rule. While wishing to limit his explicit political involvement, he used his religious authority to substantially influence the political process in Iraq.

Acting as an Opposition Figure, 2010–14

After parliamentary elections in March 2010 led to a deadlock, tensions increased in Iraq, amid accusations of fraud and the specter of political violence. Sistani insisted that the results be respected and hoped that there would be no major political crisis that would require his intervention.[144] The political elite attempted to gain an endorsement for one of these outcomes: backing Maliki for a second term, supporting a new government led by Ayad Allawi, or proposing a compromise candidate (as was the wish of the Islamic Supreme Council of Iraq—the new incarnation of SCIRI—and the Sadrists). Sistani avoided taking sides and insisted that government formation was the role of the politicians; he stated that he supported inclusive government.[145] Still, international leaders—including U.S.

president Barack Obama—and Iraqi politicians called for Sistani to decisively intervene, as the deadlock dragged on for six months.[146] Substantial interference from Iran and the United States eventually forced the Sadrists and Allawi to accept a second term for Maliki, the manner of which—including the backroom deals done to force an agreement—left Sistani even more completely disillusioned with the political elite.

The political elite's months of wrangling and apparent lack of urgency also led to wide public derision. By the time the new government was formed on December 21, 2010, Iraq's legislators had been receiving salaries of up to $18,000 per month for seven months, while meeting only a handful of times for short sessions. Sistani had previously called for top officials, including the prime minister, ministers, and members of parliament, to reduce their salaries and allowances and to avoid focusing on personal interests.[147] These calls had fallen on deaf ears, so this time Sistani insisted that a law be introduced to these effects, and for unnecessary positions and appointments to be avoided in order to reduce the waste of public funds. Yet the government formation of December 2010 led to forty-two cabinet posts and three vice presidents, and Sistani was angered that his advice was being ignored. He decided to completely stop receiving Iraqi politicians at his home from January 2011, as a signal of his frustration.

Sistani's attitude became even more critical after the government used violence to subdue nationwide protests on February 25, 2011.[148] Sistani released a statement telling the government it needed to show progress on improving services and combating corruption, and again called for reducing the costly privileges of top officials.[149] In the days after the protests, Sistani's boycott of Iraqi politicians became apparent.[150] One of the vice presidents, Adil Abdul-Mahdi, resigned in May 2011 due to Sistani's criticisms.[151] Sistani continued to insist that the wasteful spending on salaries, allowances, and privileges be reduced as a gesture to the Iraqi public that politicians were serious about reforms.[152] By August 2011, Sistani had effectively become the political opposition, letting it be known, via comments to the media from unnamed sources in his office, that politicians were not listening to his advice and instructions.[153]

Throughout the next two and a half years, Sistani became increasingly critical of the government and the wider political elite over their failings and the deterioration of the general situation in Iraq.[154] He may have felt betrayed—that those who rose to the top of politics off the back of his support now refused to heed his words and had become part of the problem. According to sources close to Sistani: "Those who stated allegiance to Sistani, who owe their position to him, when they felt that the matter had reached their pockets, they refrained from carrying out his instructions. . . . The MPs who got to parliament on the back of his name were obeying him when obedience was in their interest, but when they felt that sacrifices were required of them, they abandoned him."[155]

This dramatic change in the space of a few years, in which politicians went from seeking out Sistani's instructions to ignoring them, undoubtedly hurt Sistani and led him to undertake changes in order to preserve his political capital. One of these was to stop meeting with Iraqi officials and politicians, while at the same time continuing to meet with foreign officials and dignitaries, thereby depriving the political elite of any legitimacy by association with him.[156] In addition, the tone of his messages delivered through the Friday prayers issued from his office was consistently critical of the political elite for failing to take responsibility.[157] This showed that, while he boycotted the politicians, he was not abandoning the political process, and was still keen to press for reform of the system.[158] But his stance led to enmity from the government, particularly Maliki and his coalition, who felt threatened by Sistani's opposition and saw it as a potential block to another term.[159]

Despite the increasing level of instability throughout 2013 and into 2014, which saw the Maliki government struggle with the rise of the Islamic State, Sistani did not intervene. His view was that legitimate change could only occur through the will of the people, and they had chosen parliamentary democracy as the vehicle for that will. He articulated this view in response to a question about whether he was equally neutral toward the politicians who did their jobs well and those who did not: he again encouraged people to vote and said that it was their responsibility to choose the decent and capable candidate, not his.[160]

In the lead-up to national elections in April 2014, Sistani asked people to choose wisely and not vote on the basis of sect or tribe. Many people understood this to signal his opposition to Maliki and the same type of government, especially considering that Sistani had been calling so vehemently for change.[161] One of the Friday prayer speeches delivered by Sistani's representative was explicit in this regard: "Leave those that did not bring good to this country and replace them with other people."[162] This increased the tension between Maliki's camp and Sistani, and perhaps unfairly set up Sistani as the only credible chance for preventing Maliki's third term while the rest of the political elite faced a similar scenario as in 2010, when Maliki persevered through a monthslong deadlock to retain the premiership.

Sistani was upholding his responsibility of advising and guiding. But it was up to the public to make the decisions. Despite his warnings, many of the same faces and parties prevailed in the elections, with Maliki's State of Law coalition doing particularly well and Maliki himself picking up a record amount of votes. These results led to another deadlock as he sought a third term while the other parties struggled to identify an alternative candidate.

Maliki sought Sistani's approval in a letter dated May 1, 2014, in which he wrote: "Iraq is going through a new phase that needs your care and guidance to preserve the political process from deviation or ruin." Sistani did not respond.[163] At the same time, Sistani was receiving messages from other party leaders stressing their rejection of a

third term for Maliki and demanding the nomination of a replacement for him from the National Alliance. Sistani decided to wait for
the outcome of the dialogues of the political blocs. He informed the
representative of the UN secretary-general that he would not intervene in the matter of forming the next government unless there was
a prolonged political impasse and the country faced a suffocating
crisis that threatened the entire political process.[164]

ISIS Exposes Failures

The fall of Mosul to the Islamic State on June 10, and the subsequent
progress of the extremist group to the outskirts of Baghdad showed
how close the country was to collapse, and laid bare the failings of
the government. Iraq faced tremendous internal challenges and was
isolated internationally, as no foreign states, aside from Iran, were
willing to provide help.

On June 13, Sistani issued a fatwa for defensive jihad (though he
did not use the term "jihad") to confront the Islamic State, which gal-
vanized the war effort. It also essentially took the impetus away from
Maliki as commander in chief; Maliki was seen as being responsible
for the collapse of the security forces.

On June 20, Sistani also delivered another signal to the State
of Law coalition and other parties, indicating that they needed to
quickly form a new government with a new prime minister. The
message was delivered in another Friday prayer speech: "It is necessary for the winning blocs to engage in dialogue so that [there is]
the formation of an effective government that enjoys broad national
acceptance and rectifies previous mistakes."[165]

The pressure led to a meeting of leaders in the Dawa Party, to
which Maliki belonged, on June 23. They agreed to send a letter
to Sistani asking for his advice on what to do, given the fact that
their electoral coalition had won the most seats and had the right
to renominate Maliki as prime minister. "We look forward to your
directives and instructions," the letter said. "And we pledge to you

that we are dependent on you in all sincerity in all the issues raised and in all positions and offices, because we realize the depth of your view and based on our understanding of the religious responsibility [upon us]." Essentially, the letter was seeking a religious legal reasoning for why Maliki should not have been the prime minister. On July 10, Sistani sent a carefully worded response that gave his opinion but stopped short of a fatwa calling for Maliki's removal: "I see the need to expedite the selection of a new prime minister who enjoys broad national acceptance and who is able to work together with the political leaders of the rest of the components to save the country from the dangers of terrorism, sectarian war, and division."[166]

While this ought to have resolved the matter, Maliki suppressed the release of the letter and refused to give in. For the next month, he ignored the wishes of his own party and the wider National Alliance of Shia parties to step down. Maliki even ignored UN secretary-general Ban Ki-moon, who stated that elections by themselves "do not give full authority or legitimacy."[167]

Pushing Maliki Out

In his July 25, 2014 Friday prayer speech, Sistani hinted that Maliki needed to face reality: "The concerned parties must show a spirit of national responsibility," he stated, "which requires recognizing the principle of sacrifice and self-denial, and not clinging to positions and posts, but rather dealing realistically and flexibly with the internal and external political situation and putting the interests of the country and the Iraqi people ahead of some personal political gains."[168]

But the stalemate dragged on, with Maliki unwilling to compromise given his view that he had won elections and had the legitimate right to retain the premiership. (His electoral alliance had gained the largest number of seats but not enough to form a government by itself.)

On August 10, Maliki delivered an angry televised statement claiming that the president, Fuad Masum, had violated the constitution by failing to nominate a prime minister within the designated deadline; Maliki said he had lodged a case against Masum in the Supreme Court.[169]

This attack from Maliki spurred the president, the speaker of parliament, leaders of the Dawa Party, and others from the National Alliance into action. The next day, Masum asked Haider al-Abadi, one of the senior leaders of the Dawa Party, to form the government as the next prime minister.[170] Abadi was backed by 128 members of parliament from the National Alliance, while 52 continued to support Maliki.[171]

Alarmingly, Maliki had already mobilized troops in and around the Green Zone, the home of Iraq's government, parliament, and supreme court. Some saw this as preparations for a coup, but military officials assured the president and Abadi, the prime minister-designate, that they would not stand with Maliki.[172]

On August 12, Maliki lodged a new case in the supreme court challenging Abadi's nomination, but was shocked to find that Iran had welcomed Abadi's designation.[173] The next day, Maliki reiterated that he would not step down, and said that Abadi's appointment had no value.[174] That night, the Dawa Party leaked the letter from Sistani in the hope that Maliki would accept his fate. But he would not relent. Finally, on August 14, Maliki received a message that Sistani would explicitly call for his removal in the next day's Friday prayer speech, which finally forced Maliki into submission.[175]

Sistani had used his informal political power to force Maliki out while remaining outside politics formally and retaining independence from the state. This incident highlighted how fraught with risks the intervention of the marja is in politics. Further, while it underlined Sistani's power, the incident also showed its limits.[176]

After a few years of a reduced profile in politics, forcing the change of prime minister and issuing the jihad fatwa reasserted Sistani's importance in Iraq and his political role. The fact that the international community—including the United States, the UN, and Iran—had all turned to Sistani to resolve both crises also gave his marja'iyya unprecedented recognition.[177] In this regard, Sistani had elevated the position of marja, while still maintaining the primacy and legitimacy of the people's will and the democratic process. Importantly, Sistani's intervention did not undermine the democratic principles he worked hard to enshrine and replace them with clerical authority. He reserved his interventions for times of existential threat.

But his role as arbiter and "protector" of Iraq's democracy, using his informal power, meant that he walked a fine line, with some critics feeling he was not really neutral, and should not have such power and influence over the secular state as a religious cleric. As the scholar Caroleen Marji Sayej notes: "He tried to keep the democratic process moving in the direction that would safeguard national unity, the country's development along secular lines, and his own neutrality and independence regarding the state. He did not always succeed, yet this was an experiment after years of authoritarian rule and years of silence from the hawza." [178]

The Jihad Fatwa of 2014

The fall of Mosul, on June 10, 2014, was quickly followed in the next forty-eight hours by the massacre at Camp Speicher, an Iraqi military base, and the fall of Tikrit and other areas. The Islamic State surged to the gates of Baghdad. On June 12, videos and images began to emerge of the Islamic State capturing thousands of Iraqi Army cadets in the Speicher base near Tikrit. Islamic State media announced that the group had executed 1,700 Shia cadets and gruesome videos released later showed the massacre in detail. The impact of these three days on the Iraqi people, the security forces, and the region in general cannot be understated. The Islamic State, in its various guises, had been terrorizing rural areas in Iraq for a decade, with kidnappings, murders, and bombings interspersed with takeovers of towns and villages. But its campaigns had stepped up markedly since 2012.

The collapse of the Iraqi security forces in the face of the Islamic State onslaught led to a serious security threat that did not look like it could be stopped at the time. Foreign embassies withdrew their staff, many people became displaced as the Islamic State rolled into their towns and villages, and the Iraqi authorities faced the possibility of the collapse of the entire state with the loss of Baghdad.

The Islamic State assault led to the collapse of three Iraqi Army divisions and almost all Federal Police operating in Nineveh, Salahaddin, and Anbar governorates. The Iraqi security forces were in disarray, and it seemed the United States and other countries, including Iraq's neighbors, were not willing to intervene, despite the government asking for help.[179]

Sistani had warned the government for several years, and especially in the months leading up to June 2014, that it was risking security collapse if it did not address disenfranchisement, corruption, and lack of services for people. But the fall of Mosul was a watershed moment, and the government seemed paralyzed. At this point, Sistani began to deeply contemplate the correct course of action. The Islamic State had threatened to take over the shrine cities and was approaching Samarra, developments that harked back to the sectarian bloodletting that took place after the Askari Shrine was bombed in February 2006 by al-Qaeda. The situation was very grave and events were unfolding quickly. Sistani felt the Islamic State threat should not be underestimated.

Sistani also has a legendary grasp of history, and knew of similar instances in the past where poor governance, corruption, and unheeded warnings had led to major conflict. One event, in particular, stood out for him as having similarities, especially with the panic in Baghdad: the 1722 siege of Isfahan. In this war three centuries ago, a small, determined force of Afghan tribal warriors seized upon civil unrest, an empire in decline, and weak leadership to defeat the Persian Safavid state. The build-up to the siege reminded Sistani of current events: then as in 2014, there were ignored warnings from clerics, and a failure to prepare defense. These earlier events high-lighted to Sistani that the warning and advice of the clerics were not enough in such circumstances.

Sistani decided that if he were to intervene, then it needed to be decisive enough to change the course of events and stem the tide. Late into the night of June 12 and into the morning of June 13, he considered various options before settling on using the Friday prayer speech as the platform for his intervention.[180] He dictated to his son, Muhammad Ridha, the text of the sermon, which was then given to Abdul-Mahdi al-Karbalai, Sistani's representative in Karbala, to read out.

In the Friday sermon in Karbala on June 13, Karbalai announced a fatwa that made defense against the Islamic State a religious obligation:

> The nature of the dangers facing Iraq and its people at the present time necessitates the defense of this homeland, its people, and the honor of its citizens. This defense is a communal duty for citizens, in the sense that if sufficient people confront it so that the goal is achieved, which is to preserve Iraq, its people and its sanctities, it negates obligation for the rest. Hence, citizens who are able to bear arms and fight terrorists in defense of their country, people, and sanctities must volunteer to join the security forces.[181]

The type of fatwa was that of "sufficiency," or collective responsibility, meaning that it obliged all the faithful to heed the call, but also stipulated that, if enough people responded, the rest did not need to. The fatwa specifically called on men to volunteer for the Iraqi security forces, in defense of the nation and what they held sacred. Sistani called upon not only those Iraqis who looked to him as their spiritual guide, but also all others of any religious backgrounds and ethnicities. He issued his extraordinary decree because the situation had grown so serious—a wave of fighters was required to stem the Islamic State assault and restore confidence in the Iraqi security forces.

Interestingly, the fatwa did not use the word jihad.[182] Jihad in Shia jurisprudence refers to fighting for the cause of Islam, but Sistani was actually calling for volunteers to join state security forces and fight through that structure and chain of command. A true call to jihad would have been different, directly sanctioning Muslims to fight a holy war. Sistani's call was much broader, which is why he did not use the word jihad. However, gradual popular usage of the term *jihad fatwa* established the term as a common reference.[183]

The June 13 sermon exhorted the security forces and volunteers to defend the nation. Recognizing that the Islamic State had used fear tactics and was building momentum, Sistani wanted to turn the tide by spurring Iraqis into action: "It is not permissible for . . . fear and frustration to creep into the soul of [citizens]," Sistani stated, adding "citizens, from whom we are acquainted with patience, courage and steadfastness in such circumstances."[184] By sanctioning defensive combat, Sistani stated that any killed in the line of duty would attain the lofty religious rank of martyr: "Whoever sacrifices for the sake of defending his country, his family, and their honor, then he will be a martyr."[185]

The fatwa had the desired effect of galvanizing Iraqis to fight back against the Islamic State, and it has been credited by Iraqi and foreign leaders and officials as being the reason Baghdad did not fall.[186] Within days of this fatwa, tens of thousands of men had volunteered to join the Iraqi security forces, from a wide variety of backgrounds, nearly all of them leaving behind jobs and families to fight for the national and religious cause. Even before Sistani's fatwa, Maliki had created an official governmental body, the Popular Mobilization Commission (PMC), by executive order, in anticipation of the need to organize volunteers. The government then used this new entity to absorb the tens of thousands of new fighters into one entity. Alongside this, several existing paramilitary groups announced their mobilization as part of the PMC and moved their cadres to the front lines.

The Popular Mobilization

The organizational support that the PMC provided to these new units and fighters was limited, and many simply ended up operating as paramilitary forces, known collectively as *al-hashd al-sha'abi*, or Popular Mobilization Units (PMU). While they successfully banded together to repel the Islamic State, they have since become problematic for Iraq, representing a type of hybrid actor with one foot in the state and one foot out. Today, long after the Islamic State has been all but driven from Iraqi territory, some these forces still have their own economic and political interests and agendas—which has been problematic for governance. Several groups in the PMU denote themselves as being part of the "Islamic resistance" (*al-moqawama al-islamiya*), and while their stated national allegiance is to Iraq, their religious allegiance is to Ayatollah Khamenei and not Sistani. These groups, such as Kata'eb Hezbollah and Asa'ib Ahl al-Haq, are considered by critics to be under the de facto command of Iran's Revolutionary Guard Corps rather than the Iraqi prime minister. And one of the most blistering critiques of Sistani is that he supposedly sanctioned the role of these militias.

However, this characterization of Sistani's actions and motives is simply inaccurate. Never mind that the crisis Iraq was facing called for extraordinary action—Sistani was still explicit that his call was for the strengthening of the Iraqi military, not for the creation of militias. As he said in a statement released a week after the fatwa:

> The call of the religious authority was to join the official security forces, and not to form armed militias outside the framework of the law. Its principled position on the necessity of restricting weapons in the hands of the state is clear, and since the fall of the previous regime, no one is under

the illusion that [the religious authority] supports any armed organization that is not authorized under the law. The relevant authorities must prevent illegal armed manifestations, take the initiative to organize the volunteering process, and announce specific controls for those needed by the armed forces and other security agencies.[187]

Sistani's aim was essentially to resupply the Iraqi security forces with recruits and create a patriotic motivation to defend the country against the terrorism of the Islamic State. His actions during this time have always been interpreted by Iraqi Shia as an attempt to keep Iraq united, against foreign interference from Iran, the United States, and others, to stabilize the country, and help it become a pluralistic democracy. In the Friday prayer speeches his representatives read on his behalf, and in written communications—which include advice and guidance to fighters on the front line—he has never used the term al-hashd al-sha'abi, only ever calling the fighters "volunteers." This omission is notable—it shows that Sistani does not wish to be seen as legitimizing the various groups that have separate agendas that may undermine the state.[188]

Sistani's supporters believe that he cannot be held responsible for the creation of the PMU, or how groups within it interact with the state. Nor can the state be absolved of responsibility for dealing with the repercussions of allowing paramilitary organizations to proliferate. Sistani has continually called on state security forces in all their forms to uphold the rule of law and to protect innocent civilians, while praising the sacrifices made in the battles to liberate territory from the Islamic State.[189] Even as the war against the Islamic State was coming to an end, Sistani confirmed that his fatwa obligating people to join the security forces was still in effect.[190]

The wider context in which the fatwa was delivered also needs to be assessed. At the time, several Iraqi armed groups already existed as militias outside the state's control, and were funneling recruits to Syria in contravention of the government's policy. Some of these militias had clashed with state security forces in the past, and for several years Sistani had already considered these groups a problematic affront to the state. While the language of the fatwa explicitly limits volunteers to joining state institutions by mentioning official security forces and not forming armed militias, the post-fatwa recruitment surge mostly went not to the army or police but to para-state militias—including the problematic ones. Though the government later attempted to treat these groups as state forces by including them in the PMC, the distinct identity and operational activities of these militias outside state control has persisted.

These hybrid actors' split allegiances defy Sistani's wishes, and are certainly not the outcome he had sought. Sistani wanted recruits to join the Federal Police and Army, to replenish the entire divisions that evaporated after the fall of Mosul. There is another example of intentions in this regard: four PMU brigades had pledged their allegiance to him, and in 2020 he attempted to have those brigades moved to the Ministry of Defense from the PMC, where they would be more firmly under state control.[191]

While it is true that militias have taken advantage of the fatwa to formalize and legitimize their role, even with hindsight there was not much else Sistani could do. The simple fact is, although the unintended concomitant effects of the fatwa may have been to strengthen militias, the fatwa's primary aim of reinvigorating Iraqi defense against the Islamic State and preventing the collapse of the state was fulfilled. As such, the fatwa was successful.

An Unprecedented Moment

The magnitude of the fatwa is unprecedented in the history of Shia Islam, in addition to being a defining moment in Iraq's history and the event with the most impact on current Shia politics.

While a sizeable number of the maraji were politically active and influenced events across borders, very few have issued public jihad fatwas. When assessing contemporary history there have only been a handful of jihad fatwas issued by the top maraji and seemingly only those based in Najaf:[192] In November 1908, Akhund Khurasani, along with Mirza Hussain al-Khalili and Sheikh Abdullah al-Mazandarani, decreed jihad against Muhammad Ali, the Qajari shah of Persia, for suppressing parliament and the constitution. In December 1911, Khurasani (along with other senior maraji) and Sayed Muhammad Kadhim al-Yazdi signed separate fatwas of jihad against the Italian invasion of Libya and the Russian and British invasions of Iran. In November 1914, all the major maraji in Iraq decreed jihad against the British following the invasion of Basra. In June 1920, Mirza Muhammad Taqi al-Shirazi (based in Karbala at the time) made it permissible for people in Iraq to use force against the British in calling for their rights. In August 1920, Sheikh al-Sharia al-Isfahani issued a fatwa for jihad against the British in defense of the nation and to gain independence for Iraq. In July and August 1937, several maraji in Najaf issued jihad fatwas against the Zionists in Palestine. In August 1938 (and again in September 1947), Ayatollah Muhammad Hussain Kashif al-Ghita issued a fatwa for jihad in Palestine.[193] In June 1967, Ayatollah Muhsin al-Hakim issued a fatwa calling for jihad against Israel.

Part of why jihad fatwas are rare are debates over whether a mujtahid has the authority to issue such a fatwa, whether there is a distinction between offensive and defensive jihad, to whom and to what extent the fatwa applies, and whether another mujtahid can invalidate it. These debates stem from the subject of wilayah—the powers the maraji have as the Imam's indirect deputies—and are at the heart of the controversy surrounding Islamic government.[194]

Sistani's position in Iraq as the unrivaled supreme marja helps to solidify his authority, which is why he is more willing to issue fatwas than is perhaps his nature. The political freedom he possesses compared to his predecessors also encourages intervention, particularly as Sistani believes it is his obligation to respond to queries of a political nature.[195]

Guide and Critic, 2014–23

After Haider al-Abadi was sworn in as the new prime minister in September 2014, Sistani began to meet with politicians in the new government in the hope that they would be more willing to listen and make urgent decisions given the seriousness of Iraq's situation.[196] Sistani's representatives in Karbala also regularly met with ministers, government officials, and politicians.

Maliki had resisted giving up the premiership after the April elections, and only finally stepped down after the leak of a private letter from Sistani that urged him to accept the election results. Now, Sistani gave support to the new Abadi government, and even involved himself in Iraq's international relations. In a meeting with President Fuad Masum on November 11, Sistani passed the president a message for the Saudi leadership, whom Masum was due to meet in Riyadh three days later. (Sistani has often favored such indirect modes of communication.) In the message, the ayatollah called for strengthening of relations between the two countries, assuring the Saudis that there was no Shia position against Saudi Arabia.[197] The Saudis responded positively, and this gave the Abadi government the platform to renew the relationship.

In the first six months of the new government, Sistani used meetings and Friday prayer speeches to focus on maintaining support for the war effort while he waited to see what reforms the prime minister was undertaking. Abadi visited Sistani in April 2015 and complained to him that the political elite would not cooperate on pushing through reforms, and that he had struggled to make significant changes. (Sistani had pressed Abadi on a variety of reforms, including reducing the salaries and privileges of senior civil servants, ending the control of parties over ministries and important public institutions, and cutting down on waste of public funds and bureaucratic inefficiency.) Sistani told him to be bold and forthright with the Iraqi people so that it would be awkward for the parties to be seen as blocking reforms.

But the next couple of months passed without much progress, and as the July heat kicked in and the dismal electricity service failed again, protests broke out in Baghdad and several cities in the south. Anger and discontent focused on the poor performance of local governments. Protesters called for corruption to be rooted out.[198] Sistani warned Abadi that blaming previous governments for poor services was not enough, particularly the lack of electricity in the traditional summer heat.[199] After three weeks, Abadi had only limited reactions to the protests, and Sistani once again felt it was necessary to speak out in a very direct manner.

The marja again chose the Friday prayer sermon as the platform for his intervention. On August 7, he published his most forceful public address to date calling for immediate reforms. He also indicated his continued support for Abadi, but also warned that patience was wearing thin.

The sermon began by making clear who was to blame for Iraq's poor state of affairs: "The political forces . . . [that] hold the reins of power and decision-making through the council of representatives, the central government, and local governments bear most of the responsibility for the past problems and what the country suffers from today, and they must be aware of the danger of continuing in this situation and not developing fundamental solutions to the problems of citizens who were patient for a long time."[200]

The sermon continued by validating people's anger: "The people who endured hardships, defied car bombs, participated in the elections, and chose those who hold power from among the political forces, expect them, and rightly so, to work diligently in order to provide them with a decent life, and to do their utmost to combat corruption and achieve social justice."

Sistani then addressed the prime minister directly—something the cleric had never done before—urging him to strike corruption with an iron fist: "What is expected of the prime minister, who is the top executive official in the country and who has shown interest in the people's demands and his eagerness to implement them, is to be more daring and courageous in his reform steps . . . to take important decisions and strict measures in the field of combating corruption and achieving social justice, and to strike with an iron fist those who tamper with the people's wealth."

Sistani went on to implore Abadi to "transcend partisan and sectarian quotas and the like in order to reform state institutions." He continued: "[The prime minister] should seek to appoint the right person in the right place, even if they do not belong to any of the ruling parties, regardless of their sectarian or ethnic affiliation, and [should] not hesitate to remove those who are not in the right place even if they are supported by some political forces." Sistani concluded by telling Abadi that he should not be afraid of those political forces, but should rather rely on God "and on the honorable people who want this from him and will support and back him in achieving that."

Disappointment

The tone, manner, and instructions of Sistani's August 7, 2015 address are all important. In it, he positioned the marja above the state, as a guide, but in a much more forceful way than might have been expected given his past activities. As it turned out, however, the sermon was the highpoint of Sistani's public interaction with the state, which came at a moment when he felt real reform was possible and his words could give the push needed. But disappointment followed.

Within two days of Sistani's call, the government announced some austerity measures aimed at the political elite.[201] As people welcomed the decisions and momentum continued to build for reform, the parties in parliament felt the pressure to accede to the reforms. They voted to approve Abadi's measures and to give him a mandate to undertake them. Abadi continued to announce more reform measures in the following weeks.

However, these reforms had only limited implementation, and the parties began to push back. At the same time, Sistani said that the measures were not the deep reforms that were required, though he held out hope the measures were a prelude to change.[202] But no real reforms were forthcoming, and as protests disappeared and pressure receded, parliament revoked Abadi's mandate. In the end, many of the reforms that Abadi had announced never happened.[203]

This deeply disappointed Sistani, who sensed that his words were going unheeded, and that Iraq was heading to a disaster.[204] The ayatollah began to limit his direct interaction with politicians once again. When Abadi visited Najaf on November 5, 2015, the prime minister was able to meet with the other three senior maraji, but Sistani would not grant him an audience.

In a sermon published on January 8, 2016, Sistani went public with his disappointment: "Last year, over a period of several months, we called in our Friday sermons . . . [for] serious steps in the path of real reform, achieving social justice, combating corruption, and prosecuting the corrupt, but the year passed and nothing clear was achieved on the ground, and this is a matter of great regret."[205]

Then came the sermon of January 22, 2016, which Sistani delivered with words of exhaustion and frustration: "Our voices went hoarse, without effect, with repeated calls . . . for officials and the political forces that hold the reins of affairs to be aware of the size of the responsibility placed on their shoulders, and to renounce political differences behind which there are only personal, factional, and regional interests."[206]

By the beginning of February 2016, Sistani had decided that the politicians were not listening and that reforms were not going to happen. He again repositioned himself away from the political elite, refusing to meet with them and even deciding to mostly forgo commenting weekly on current affairs in the Friday prayer speeches.[207] He had returned to his posture of 2011–14, when he had assumed the stance of political opposition to the government, but opposition in the form of disengagement—an effective boycott.

Weeks after Sistani stopped publicly focusing on politics, protests started again, this time with Sadrist backing of the protests and eventually with the participation of Muqtada al-Sadr himself.[208] Even as the protests grew and overran the Green Zone, Sistani was unmoved to comment or intervene. On May 4, 2016, after protesters stormed parliament, Sistani's office simply released a brief statement stating that he was closely watching the situation. The office called on all sides to "think carefully about the future of the people and take serious and tangible steps to get out of the current situation into a better future."[209] The head of the UN mission in Iraq, Ján Kubiš, met Sistani on May 30, 2016. "The marja'iyya is following very, very carefully what is happening and will intervene whenever that is necessary," Kubiš reported after the meeting.[210] For his part, Abadi visited Najaf on June 22, 2016, but was unable to get a meeting with Sistani, a fact that highlighted Sistani's efforts to distance himself from the political elite.[211] Abadi knew Sistani had more to offer on the political situation, but no public comment was forthcoming. This highlights Sistani's sensitivity to the prevalent context and conditions upon which his interventions are predicated and whether an intervention will be successful or not.

Guiding from a Distance

For the next two years, Sistani did not receive Iraqi politicians and seldom commented on political issues. This stance, from early 2016 to mid 2018, was meant to show his displeasure with the political elite and the lack of reforms. Yet he did not totally ignore state affairs. In sermons, he continued to press for protecting citizens in the liberation effort and respect for human rights when the Mosul campaign against the Islamic State began in October 2016.[212] And after the Kurdistan Regional Government (KRG) organized a referendum on independence in September 2017, Sistani reacted critically.[213]

Further, when federal forces retook control of Kirkuk from the Islamic State in October 2017, leading to heightened tensions between the KRG and the central government, Sistani cautioned against a divisive or sectarian view of the events.[214] In another sermon, on December 15, 2017, after the war against the Islamic State was declared to be over, Sistani said: "The battle against corruption—which has been delayed for a long time—is no less ferocious than the battle against terrorism, if not more severe."[215]

The build-up to parliamentary elections in May 2018 saw fragmentation increase within and between parties and political coalitions. Economic conditions had not noticeably improved, and a young population was ever more disenchanted by the political elite and the post-2003 system. Sensing the apathy, Sistani released a long statement for Friday prayers on May 4, 2018, a little more than a week before national elections, outlining his view on the political situation.[216]

First, he explained why he viewed parliamentary democracy as the most suitable choice for Iraq's political system: "Since the fall of the former authoritarian regime, the religious authority has sought to replace it with a system that adopts political pluralism and the peaceful transfer of power by referring to the ballot boxes, in periodic, free and fair elections, in the belief that there is no alternative to following this path in governing the country. . . . The religious authority still holds the opinion that following this path constitutes—in principle—the correct and appropriate choice for the country's present and future."

Next, Sistani described the conditions for elections to work well: "That the electoral law be fair, respecting the sanctity of the vote and not allowing circumvention of it. Including: that the electoral lists compete on economic, educational, and service programs that can be implemented away from personalization, ethnic or sectarian rhetoric, and media one-upmanship." He also cautioned against "external interference in the matter of elections, whether by financial or other support." He added that voters needed to be aware of "the value of their votes and their important role in shaping the future of the country, so they do not give them to unqualified people for a cheap price, or follow whims and emotions, or care for personal interests, tribal tendencies, or the like."

Next, Sistani addressed why apathy had set in among voters:

It is certain that the failures that accompanied past electoral experiences—from the misuse of power by many of those who were elected or assumed high positions in the government, their contribution to spreading corruption and wasting public money in an unprecedented way, distinguishing themselves with large salaries and allocations, and their failure to perform their duties in the service of the people and providing a decent life for the people—was only a natural result of not applying many of the necessary conditions—albeit to varying degrees—when holding those elections.

Sistani went on to talk about the responsibility of voting, though he stopped short of calling it an obligation:

Participation in these elections is a right for every citizen who fulfills the legal conditions, and there is nothing obligating [citizens] to exercise this right except what they are convinced of in the requirements of the supreme interest of the people and this country. Yes, they should pay attention to the fact that relinquishment of exercising the electoral right gives an additional opportunity for others to have their elected representatives win parliamentary seats . . . but in the end, the decision to participate or not remains up to the voter alone."

Despite Sistani's warnings about the repercussions of voter apathy, the elections had a low turnout and the predictable months-long process to form a new coalition government followed. Even though he had made it clear that he did not endorse any party or candidate, popular expectations increased that Sistani would resolve the stand-off over who would become the prime minister.

But Sistani didn't choose a winner—at least not exactly. Instead, he withheld endorsements and gave veiled criticisms. Abadi's bloc, the Victory Alliance, had fared poorly in the elections, and his chances of continuing as prime minister were slim. But when Sistani's representative criticized the government in the July 27, 2018 prayer speech, Abadi's fortunes were sealed: his term was over.[217] However, Sistani's office also effectively ruled out other senior politicians with a statement on September 9, 2018: "The marja'iyya . . . does not support the next prime minister if he is chosen from among the politicians who were in power in the past years."[218]

Nudging for Reform

Though Sistani generally does not endorse or nominate any politicians for top posts, he sometimes does try to encourage consensus when there is a deadlock. This is especially true when it comes to the issue of the premiership, where the Shia parties compete intensely to gain the post, but mostly settle on a compromise.

According to Sistani's representative in Lebanon, the marja'iyya "intervenes whenever it senses danger imminent in Iraq and the interests of its people, and finds that its intervention is useful in resolving or mitigating intractable crises, and the intervention of the marja'iyya—which is keen not to exceed the legal frameworks—is, in various declared and unannounced forms, depending on circumstances."[219]

For weeks after the official election results were announced in August 2018—almost two months after election day—Iraq's parties failed to form a government and select a prime minister. At this point, of the possible choices, Sistani preferred Adil Abdul-Mahdi, with whom he maintained a respectful relationship, and discreetly informed Muqtada al-Sadr, whose party held the crucial seats required, that he would be amenable to such a nominee.[220] So, on October 2, 2018, Abdul-Mahdi was nominated as prime minister, and Sistani once again hoped that a new government would finally deliver positive results in terms of the kinds of reforms he had long sought.

During this time, Sistani continued to refuse to meet with Iraqi officials and kept his political comments limited, but he did receive foreign officials, and he sometimes used these meetings to convey messages to domestic leaders.[221] In a November 2018 meeting with Kubiš, who was now the outgoing head of the UN mission, Sistani said he was "waiting to see the outlines of success in [government] work."[222] On February 6, 2019, Sistani received the new head of the UN Mission in Iraq, Jeanine Hennis-Plasschaert, and used the occasion to urge the government to show quick progress. "If the political blocs do not change their approach in dealing with the country's issues," Sistani warned, "there will be no real opportunity to resolve the current crises."[223]

Yet again, however, the political elite stifled any real improvement in the general situation, by preventing significant reforms, increasing public spending without a clear economic plan, and failing to tackle corruption. In the June 14, 2019 Friday prayer speech, Sistani expressed his dismay:

> The dispute broke out again— at times openly and hidden at others—among the parties that hold the reins, and the conflict aggravated between forces that want to preserve their previous positions and other forces that emerged during the war with the Islamic State seeking to perpetuate their presence and obtain certain gains, and the struggle for positions continues . . . and the rampant corruption in state institutions has not yet been met with clear practical steps to reduce it and hold those involved in it accountable.[224]

Sistani predicted, as he had in 2015, that the popular calls for reform would grow louder: "Those who oppose reform, and are betting that the demands for it will diminish, must know that reform is an inevitable necessity, and if the manifestations of the demand for it diminish for a while, then they will return at another time with a much stronger and broader scope, and it will be too late for regrets."[225]

The Tishreen Movement

The Abdul-Mahdi government turned out to be another disappointment. Sistani had expected more urgency from Abdul-Mahdi and better performance from him as prime minister, but was surprised that he was not up to the task. When protests broke out on October 1, 2019—in what would come to be known as the Tishreen movement—and the security forces reacted violently to them, Sistani responded with a statement in the October 2019 Friday prayer. In the statement, he criticized the government and the political elite, warning them to "rectify matters before it is too late."[226] For the next four months, Sistani returned to using the weekly Friday prayer sermon as his platform to comment on political affairs, as the reaction to protests escalated into a crisis and larger numbers took to the streets. Sistani held the government responsible for the bloody violence: "The government and its security apparatus are responsible for the heavy bloodshed in the demonstrations of the past days," he said in his October 11 sermon.[227] He continued to press for protecting the demonstrations and for the political elite to listen to the protesters' demands, but his words went unheeded.[228]

The violent reaction of the dominant political forces to the Tishreen movement, and the lack of reforms on the horizon, completely disillusioned Sistani in the entire political class. He was resigned to the fact that the state in its current form would not improve its governance, nor would the parties change their behavior. These failures were a deeply painful blow to his aspirations for Iraq. He also felt personally betrayed by those politicians and leaders from whom he had expected so much better, and to whom he had given ample support.[229]

In a November 11, 2019 meeting with Hennis-Plasschaert, Sistani referred to "his repeated warning several years ago of the dangers of exacerbating financial and administrative corruption, poor public services, and the absence of social justice." But, Sistani said, he had not found "ears willing to listen among officials to address this."[230] Sistani went on: "the relevant authorities do not have enough seriousness in implementing any real reform." To reflect his utter disapproval, Sistani even suggested considering other options in dealing with the state. "If the three executive, legislative, and judicial authorities are not able to carry out the necessary reforms or do not want to do so," he said, "then another path must be considered . . . because the situation cannot continue as it was before the recent protests."

The alternative path Sistani alluded to here is a complete change in the political system in Iraq, to a new structure or form of government different from the post-2005 one—though he has not described in greater detail what such a new system might look like, or how it could be achieved. Even today, Sistani continues to warn that the Tishreen protests were a watershed moment, and the political elite cannot continue as if nothing happened.

Islamic Democracy

In the Friday prayer speech of November 15, 2019, Sistani defined his view of the government's authority, in light of what might be called Islamic democracy: "The government derives its legitimacy—in other than tyrannical regimes and the like—only from the people, and there is no one else to grant it legitimacy. The will of the people is represented in the result of a secret general ballot, if it is conducted fairly and impartially."[231] This is perhaps the clearest opinion of a Shia marja on democracy, and is at the heart of Sistani's view on the sovereignty of the people.

Government security forces continued to repress protests and, after a particularly bloody day in Nasiriyah on November 28, 2019, Sistani forced Abdul-Mahdi's resignation by urging parliament to reconsider support for his government.[232] This intervention, which was again made via a Friday sermon, was balanced with a comment on the limits of the marja'iyya and its political role. "The religious authority will remain a support for the honorable Iraqi people," he stated. "It has nothing but advice and guidance as to what it deems to be in the interest of the people, and it remains for the people to choose what they deem to be the best for their present and future without guardianship over them." Abdul-Mahdi announced his resignation the next day.

Instability continued to prevail in the following weeks, and while Sistani kept up his advice and warnings the reality was that they had limited impact on events. In several statements, Sistani had warned about foreign interference in political and security affairs and the need to protect Iraq's sovereignty, but the situation became dangerous in the days preceding and after the assassination of Qassem Soleimani and Abu Mahdi al-Muhandis on January 3, 2020.[233] Sistani was highly critical of the assassination and sent a letter of condolence to Ali Khamenei, Iran's supreme leader.[234]

After four months of protests, repression and violent attempts to end the demonstrations with no new government yet in place, on January 31, 2020, Sistani intervened by calling for early elections. He was recovering from an operation on a broken femur, sustained in a fall at home, but was still forceful in his Friday sermon that day.[235] "It is imperative to quickly hold early elections so that the people can have their say, and the next parliament emanates from their free will and is concerned with taking the necessary steps for reform and issuing critical decisions that determine the future of the country," he stated.[236] The following week's Friday prayer sermon, on February 7, repeated the call for early elections to be held "in a reassuring atmosphere without the side effects of money or illegal weapons or external interference."[237]

The February 7, 2020 sermon was the last Friday prayer sermon to include a political statement by Sistani, and marked the beginning of reduced involvement by Sistani in politics, which continues today. Sistani had begun to feel his words were having little effect and that it was time for the political elite to take full responsibility for their actions without any further advice from him.[238] In some ways, this new attitude is similar to the opposition-through-disengagement stance he adopted in 2011–14.

Political Semiretirement

Friday prayers at the Imam Hussain shrine in Karbala were suspended because of COVID-19 on February 28, 2020, and have not resumed.[239] Since the beginning of the pandemic, Sistani has only communicated with the public through rare statements posted on his official website. In effect, March 2020 was the start of Sistani's semiretirement politically. For the rest of 2020, Sistani mainly issued directives and rulings on how the COVID-19 pandemic should be dealt with.[240] Sistani's disappointment with Adil Abdul-Mahdi's performance meant that he did not engage with the process of choosing a successor, and he generally kept a distance from the government of Mustafa al-Kadhimi (prime minister from May 2020 until October 2022).

Sistani's representative later explained, in April 2022, why he stopped issuing Friday prayer speeches: "Some political entities were not responding to much of what the religious authority indicated," he said in a statement, and noted that "the supreme marja'iyya does not only want to preach. Rather, it wants the speech to have an impact. And some of [the political parties'] response was very weak, even with the content of the sermon being repeated more than once."[241]

Nearly a year after the October 2019 protests, a date had still not been set for early elections that protesters demanded. When Sistani met with Hennis-Plasschaert again on September 13, 2020, he called for an end to the delay in holding the elections.[242]

Sistani also made several other notable comments in that meeting. First, he insisted that elections be conducted "according to a fair and just law, far from the private interests of some blocs and political parties." These interests had forced parliament to adopt district-level voting in the election law for the first time, against the preference of most parties.

Second, he called for the elections to be "supervised and monitored in coordination with the relevant department in the United Nations mission." This appeal foreshadowed the contestation of election results by the Shia Coordination Framework, a political bloc, in October 2021.

Third, Sistani reiterated the importance of parliamentary democracy. However, he clarified that the goal was not elections in and of themselves, but rather the outcomes they should lead to if conducted properly. "Early elections are not an end in themselves," he said, "but rather the correct peaceful path out of the current impasse from which the country is suffering." These statements repeated his conviction that the people are sovereign, and that parliamentary democracy is the best form of governance for Iraq.

Fourth, Sistani gave the new government some backing and urged it to push ahead with imposing the rule of law: "The current government is called upon to continue and proceed decisively and forcefully with the steps it has taken in order to implement social justice, control the border crossings, improve the performance of the security forces so that they are characterized by a high degree of discipline and professionalism, impose the prestige of the state, withdraw unauthorized weapons from it, and not allow the division of areas in the country into zones that are controlled by certain groups by force of arms under different titles, who do not uphold the applicable laws." (The latter part of this statement was a veiled reference to groups in the PMU.)

Cultivating a Broader Appeal

One of the most significant moments in the centuries-long history of the marja'iyya occurred on March 6, 2021, with Pope Francis's visit to Sistani.[243] It was the first time that a pope had visited Iraq, and his meeting with Sistani emphasized the ayatollah's position as the preeminent religious authority in Shia Islam, as well as his unique influence in Iraq. It also placed greater emphasis on Sistani's role as a leader of faith and a force for better communal relations, rather than that of political referee. The warm meeting, in which the two leaders held hands, was a show of solidarity by Sistani to Iraq's Christians, and highlighted his respect for other faiths and pluralism in general.[244] The pope thanked Sistani "for speaking up in defense of those most vulnerable and persecuted amid the violence and great hardships."[245] The meeting also reinforced Sistani's international credentials as a man of peace. By making the trip to Najaf, Pope Francis showed that in Sistani he had, in the words of a *New York Times* story on the meeting, an "ideal interlocutor . . . holy, credible and powerful."[246] The pope was glowing in his praise of Sistani: "I felt the duty . . . to go and see a great, a wise man, a man of God: only by listening to him do you perceive this. . . . He is a person who has that wisdom and also prudence . . . and he was very respectful in the meeting. I felt honored . . . a humble and wise man, it did good to my soul this meeting. He is a beacon of light."[247] The two have maintained a good relationship since their meeting, exchanging letters that touched on the issues of faith, peace, and rights.[248]

Ahead of the elections scheduled for October 2021, many in Iraq expected voter turnout to be low. But again, Sistani encouraged "everyone to participate consciously and responsibly in the upcoming elections, although they are not devoid of some shortcomings." As in the past, he admonished voters to "take lessons from past experiences and be aware of the value of their votes and their important role in shaping the country's future."[249]

The election results were intensely contested and, once again, a long period of bitter divisions and heated negotiations over government formation set in. Sistani was adamant that he would not intervene this time, no matter how complicated the situation became.[250] This position was based on his experience and belief that all sides in the political arena were to blame for the country's ills and that none were willing to listen.

Even when Sadrist protests escalated into occupying parliament and, later, into violent clashes with opponents from the Shia Coordination Framework in the Green Zone in August 2022, Sistani refused to publicly intervene.[251] (Though some believe Sistani communicated to Sadr the need to prevent further violence after the events of August 29, 2022, in which at least thirty people were killed, it is unlikely that Sistani did so directly.[252]) Not intervening even at moments of high crisis may point to an evolution of Sistani's strategy to push the political elite to reform—to show that he will no longer work to prevent escalations and leave the politicians (and the public) to deal with their choices, as grave as the consequences may be.

The acrimonious year-long process to form a government validated Sistani's stance: Despite repeated calls from various sides for him to broker a consensus, it turned out that the disputes were so bitter that his intervention would not have helped or been effective. It was better for him to stay out of it completely. His commitment to this approach reflects his desire to protect his legacy and political capital, while also acknowledging that the marja cannot continuously intervene in messy political situations, and that politics and government is primarily the domain and responsibility of politicians. Sistani has made this argument before, and after twenty years of the new Iraq he firmly believes its politicians should be held accountable, and the marja'iyya's need to guide and intervene is much less than it used to be, especially if it falls on deaf ears.[253]

However, Sistani still engages with foreign dignitaries; such engagement reflects the marja's transnational role and his duty of care to Shia communities across the world, in addition to dealing with matters beyond the political confrontations in Iraq. An example of this is Sistani's meeting with the high representative for the UN Alliance of Civilizations, Miguel Moratinos, on December 7, 2022, to discuss interreligious dialogue and the protection of religious sites.[254] Another is Sistani's December 19, 2022 meeting with Christian Ritscher, a UN special advisor and the head of UNITAD (the UN Investigative Team to Promote Accountability for Crimes Committed by Da'esh/ISIL).[255]

Sistani also released a statement on February 7, 2023, concerning the earthquake that hit Turkey and Syria, which shows the continued transnational and humanitarian interests of the marja'iyya.[256] On June 29, 2023, in response to a protest in Sweden in which the Quran was burned, Sistani's office released a letter addressed to the UN secretary-general, António Guterres, urging the UN to take "active steps to prevent the recurrence of such cases and prompting states to reconsider the legislation that allows their occurrence."[257]

The Pillar of the People's Sovereignty

Iraq's next scheduled parliamentary elections are due to take place by October 2025, and it could be that events until then do not require Sistani to comment or to intervene on political issues. At the time of writing, Sistani is still receiving believers and well-wishers almost daily, but has kept up his boycott of Iraqi politicians and is still seen as a critic of the political elite and as being in opposition to them. Sistani is still assessing the current government of Prime Minister Mohammed Shia al-Sudani, but so far, no major criticism of it has emerged from Najaf. For now, Sistani's political role is much less active than it used to be, but he still maintains a close eye on political affairs.

Whatever the next few years hold in store, the decade since Sistani's so-called jihad fatwa—the call to arms against the Islamic State—has solidified his stature in the history of Iraq and in the history of Shia Islam. He has skillfully deployed his charismatic, traditional, and rational-legal authority at various junctures to influence Iraqi affairs, but without ever overstepping the boundaries of his own apparent philosophy of influence rather than control, or observation rather than supervision.

Enduring Capital

Returning to political capital as the unit of analysis in this work and the views of Weber on authority, after having documented Sistani's actions, we can now reflect on occasions where he deployed his charismatic, traditional, and rational-legal authority. He used his charismatic authority to mobilize Iraqis to protest against Bremer's plan to impose a constitution and also to turn out to vote three times in 2005 in legislative elections and the constitutional referendum. He used his traditional authority by consolidating control of the marja'iyya and the shrines, and expanding the influence of the Najaf hawza. He used the rational-legal authority by issuing the fatwa to defend against the Islamic State and in approval for the Shia Endowment Law which confirmed the authority of the supreme marja in Najaf.

Using Bourdieu's framework for capital, we can also highlight four instances in very different situations where Sistani used his power, his religious, cultural, social and symbolic capital, in very different ways. The first example was Sistani's very cautious and highly defensive approach to the violent authoritarianism of the Ba'ath regime. Second was Sistani's reluctant moves against Bremer, where, because his views and those of the Iraqi people were not taken seriously, Sistani had to mobilize his supporters to make sure democracy was defended. The third use of his capital was in the run-up to the January 2005 elections, where he deployed his considerable religious, cultural, social and symbolic capital to support the formation of the UIA ahead of the elections. The fourth instance where he used his power was in his attempts to restrict the abuses of power in Iraq's political system and reform its function.

The application of these two frameworks to Sistani's career as a religious authority confirm that Sistani is a major political actor who utilized authority and capital in various forms and in varying circumstances. That he was able to do so with such impact and maintain his power for so long reflects that he has been an exceptional marja acting in exceptional times.

Comparing Sistani to his predecessors and other maraji shows that, on the evidence available, he has been the most impactful marja for several centuries. We cannot know how, for example, Khoei would have utilized his position had he been in Sistani's place, so the comparison is relative to the circumstances each found himself in. What we do know is Sistani did use his position and authority for immense impact, and assessing that impact shows how exceptional Sistani is.

However, it is possible to overstate Sistani's power in Iraqi politics and, given that his semiretirement in March 2020 seems to be based on his thorough disappointment at the lack of political reforms in Iraq, it is pertinent to ask whether Sistani's inability to force the political elite to change their rapacious and coercive behavior or meaningfully reform the system reflects a limit of his power or a failure in strategy. As noted earlier, some observers believed the period after 2005 showed a sustained inability by Sistani to meaningfully influence the political system and its ruling elite. Despite the direct and successful interventions he undertook, such as to block Maliki's third term and remove Abdul-Mahdi, Sistani's struggle to fundamentally improve the system he was central to creating indicates a limit to his political influence. It may be that Sistani's political influence has peaked and it will not be sustained in the way it was.

3
Najaf's Political Ideology

In this chapter, I assess Sistani's role, his political methodology, and how his model of religious authority differs from that practiced in Iran. I attempt to elucidate Sistani's political ideology or vision of political rule for Iraq, based on his statements.

Leadership and Politics

Sistani's personality is a key part of how he deals with politics. His political personality was shaped by his experiences before 1992, but even from a young age, Sistani was known to be ascetic, reclusive, and devoted to research. He mostly stayed away from the social life of the hawza and avoided taking on leadership roles. His marja'iyya is highly unusual in that he was not well known by Shia Muslims when he became a marja, he has not taught publicly for almost all of his tenure, he has not published his works on jurisprudence apart from some reports by his students, he is not outgoing and does not engage with public events, and access to him is very limited. All of these characteristics are a departure from his predecessors and from how other maraji manage their roles. Yet Sistani's different style seems not to have hindered his rise to become supreme marja. The style may also be unique to Sistani—it is unlikely that the next few generations of maraji will ascend in the same manner.

Sistani's pre-2003 approach to politics was focused on avoiding antagonizing the state, in order to protect the hawza of Najaf from repercussions. He held political views but did not offer them publicly due to the hostile authoritarian environment. Sistani knew he did not have the power to confront the regime, as his followers would not be in a position to follow through on any call he might give to confront Saddam. Thus, his obligations were to survive and give his followers a sense of solidarity in difficult times by opposing the regime in the only way he could. "The situation was very critical for His Eminence and he remained for many years a hostage in his house, exercising his responsibilities within the narrowest limits, to avoid giving any pretext to the regime's organs in a wrath against the hawza and its students," said Muhammad Ridha, Sistani's son, in February 2004. "And he succeeded—praise be to God—in preserving the entity of the holy hawza in extremely dangerous and complex circumstances."[1]

The seclusion gave Sistani time to read more about what was happening in the world and to focus on keeping the hawza of Najaf functioning despite the regime's efforts. And remaining at home with limited contact also suited his personality. He understood that his marja'iyya was restricted in Iraq, but effective abroad, and he found that to be the suitable position at the time. Sistani kept abreast of all the political developments in the region and was aware of the Iraqi opposition's activities in the lead-up to the 2003 invasion.[2]

Regime Change

Immediately after regime change in April 2003, Sistani sent a message to Ayatollah Muhammad Saeed al-Hakim in Najaf, asking Hakim to lead the Iraqi Shia, since Hakim was Iraqi and could intervene in politics more easily.[3] Hakim refused, because more people followed Sistani and said that the rest of the maraji in Najaf would back Sistani's leadership, publicly supporting him when they agreed with his stances and never disagreeing with him in public.[4] It was true, too, that many Iraqi Shia were asking for Sistani's guidance and leadership. Sistani acquiesced and accepted the role of leader, but kept the other maraji updated on his plans and made it a cooperative partnership, where possible. This cooperative attitude helped Sistani and is perhaps unmatched in the history of Najaf.

With the backing of the other maraji, and as the most widely followed marja in Iraq and abroad, Sistani was confident that his views and his fatwas would have great impact.[5] As he was the most senior religious leader in Iraq, Sistani knew he would have to intervene when necessary. This awareness of his own position caused Sistani's post-2003 approach to politics to be different. The context had changed, people wanted him to intervene and would listen to his guidance. Since his opinions would have an effect, his obligation changed to becoming more active in politics.

In general, Sistani's approach is based on having as much information as possible and full appraisal of the prevalent political conditions. Sistani utilizes sources and aides to provide him with the relevant material and background knowledge on an issue or an individual.[6] Several Iraqi politicians I have spoken to over the years said that, when they met Sistani, he had been well briefed, was aware of even the minute details of the topics at hand, and had received information about their private meetings and discussions.

Sistani's involvement in the drafts of the constitution, legislation, and other state processes is also well noted, and he uses multiple, non-linked sources to verify and cross-check information. Additionally, he is a voracious reader of newspapers, books, articles, government communiques, official proceedings, political statements, legislation, manuscripts, journals and magazines.[7]

Sistani's approach means that he is unusually well informed about affairs in Iraq, the region, and the world—much more so than

his peers and even most politicians. In that sense, he has not operated as a cloistered regionalist or been solely focused on religious
jurisprudence, as most of the maraji have tended to be. Part of the
reason for this difference is his personality and method of study,
which addresses a hunger for knowledge; another reason for the difference is the conditions he lived with in the hawza, particularly at
sensitive times such as with the ayatollahs Hussain al-Burujerdi and
Abu al-Qasim Khoei, which required him to see the role of a marja
as being bigger than just a jurisprudent.

After he collects information, Sistani then considers if he should
intervene, what the risks of doing so may be, what the best outcome
would be, and how to achieve it.[8] Sometimes, Sistani communicates
decisions through personal meetings, and others through messages
via intermediaries but also statements; he also uses his Friday prayer
speeches (delivered publicly by a representative), and public comments from his network. Not speaking out or meeting or refusing
to receive an intermediary or a letter is also a favored method to
declare a stance. There is also a nuance in his direct interventions,
sometimes in his name, sometimes in that of his office, sometimes
as a statement and, most importantly, sometimes as a fatwa. Because
of Sistani's guarded approach, many important interventions have
never occurred in public and are only known to a select few behind
the scenes. As politicians are not familiar with the informal intrica-
cies of the marja'iyya and sometimes even its language, Sistani has
used a combination of these methods to communicate with them.
Sistani's restrictions on meeting with politicians has also opened up
a role for intermediaries, able to deliver a message from Sistani discreetly, with less risks than personal meetings or public comment.
The importance of the use of informal channels by the marja'iyya
should not be underestimated.

An important factor in his decision-making is the need to preserve political capital, to avoid intervening too much, and to wait
until conditions are right so that his voice is keenly sought out and is

therefore more likely to have an effect.[9] Every statement is carefully worded, and the Sistani network is engineered to amplify his stances.

"Highly strategic" is perhaps the best description for Sistani's approach to politics. One thing Sistani is definitely not is apolitical.

Quietist or Activist?

Because Sistani's interventions are limited yet effective, he has been viewed variously as a "quietist, or as semi-quietist, or even an active cleric," in the words of Kalantari.[10] These categories are of course simplistic, but even if we do use them, Sistani could at any one time be described as one, all, or none of the above. He believes context matters—whether he has an obligation to act, whether his views will have an impact, whether the desired outcome is possible.

Sistani does not believe that clerics should be formally involved in politics, but he does believe that the religious authorities have an obligation to guide and intervene if the people want them to, and if the conditions are suitable.[11] In response to a question from the Associated Press in October 2003 about why his voice was not heard more often, Sistani's office stated: "His Eminence, despite his great interest and continuous follow-up of Iraqi affairs in all their aspects, has refrained from interfering in the details of political work, and [has always] given space for politicians whom the Iraqi people trust to exercise this task, and His Eminence is satisfied with giving advice and guidance to those who visit him and meet him."[12]

The times Sistani has chosen *not* to intervene can be as important as his interventions. For example, in 2006, after the Askari Shrine in Samarra was destroyed by al-Qaeda, Sistani would not sanction defensive volunteers to protect the other shrines and Shia communities. And in 2010, despite a deadlock and significant opposition from the other political parties to Nouri al-Maliki remaining as prime minister, Sistani chose not to intervene in the matter. So too, the year-long gridlock on government formation in the aftermath of the 2021 elections did not elicit a public stance from Sistani, nor did the violent clashes in the Green Zone in August 2022. These examples demonstrate the intentionality behind Sistani's actions, and that he employs a rationale to weigh up his positions, and acts based on a calculation that assesses risks and outcomes.

Sistani is acutely aware that he is part of a 1,000-year-old chain of maraji, and that his duty is to preserve this link of leadership. Thus, when dealing with politics, he seeks to maintain the prestige of his position, the potential impact of his actions, and the power of the marja'iyya. This means keeping the marja'iyya focused on its domain of religious authority and not diluting its power by becoming too involved in nonreligious affairs or in the modern state and its politics.

Despite ensuring the independence from the state of the hawza of Najaf and the marja'iyya, and avoiding formal involvement of the marja in politics, Sistani did agree to his role being explicitly mentioned in the Shia Endowment Law no. 57 of 2012.[13] In Article 4.2 of that law, it is stated that the head of the Shia Endowment should be appointed "after the approval of the supreme religious authority—and he is the jurist who is followed by most of the Shia in Iraq among the jurists of Najaf." Article 14 similarly describes the supreme marja's role in appointing and dismissing trustees of endowments. Article 15 states that the Shia Endowment cannot be involved in the affairs of the hawza without the approval of the supreme marja. The significance of this law is that it formalizes recognition of the supreme marja, his influence over the Shia Endowment, his control of the hawza and the shrines, and their independence from the state—and that the marja'iyya is a Najafi one.

Political Ideology and the Civil State

An important distinction should be made between what Sistani believes is applicable and suitable for the context and conditions of post-2003 Iraq, and his general theory on governance in the period of the major occultation of the Twelfth Imam.[14] This distinction reflects the methodology of Shia jurists: they exercise much intellectual freedom in their teachings and research but are more restricted in their practice.

Sistani's views on Iraq should be understood in this context: that which is suitable for Iraq in the current conditions, not necessarily what his political ideology actually is. As a jurist, Sistani has a political ideology rooted in Islamic law, but this describes a general theory of governance in a completely Islamic society. It is not applicable in Iraq's current circumstances; therefore, Sistani advocates a view that prescribes the preferred political system for Iraq in the current context. This thinking explains why, when asked whether an Islamic government in Iraq should be based on wilayat al-faqih, Sistani's response has been that it is not feasible—not that he does not believe in it.[15]

Sistani has never disclosed his political ideology, and it is difficult to infer it from his teachings, as there is limited information on his views. However, his political views on post-2003 Iraq are clearer, and though he has not explicitly articulated his approach or given it a definition, it is possible to explain it concisely based on his public comments. According to Sistani's representative in Beirut, "Sistani's attitude towards authority is better understood through his practices, rather than his legal theories."[16] Some clerics see the marja'iyya's role in political affairs as being akin to that of a doctor, intervening in moments of crisis, or acting as a spiritual father when needed.[17]

During 2003 and 2004, Sistani stated many times that the form of governance in Iraq should be determined by the Iraqi people. This is the pillar of his view: that the people's will and sovereignty are the source of legitimacy for the political system. Sistani believes his role is to support the people in making clear their will and help create the conditions for them to express it.

This pillar of people's sovereignty in Sistani's political theory for Iraq is what several writers have termed *wilayat al-umma* (authority of the people, in contrast to wilayat al-faqih) or, more accurately, *iradat al-umma* (will of the people).[18] It asserts the people's right and authority to choose a system of governance that they see fits their circumstances. When people make their choices, it legitimizes the state, and the outcomes of those choices must be adhered to. Because of the history of authoritarianism in Iraq, it was logical that people would choose a democratic system. Given that the majority are Muslims, it is natural that they want a state that respects Islamic values and principles. This is why Sistani pushed for a constitution written by Iraqis chosen through elections—he was sure of the outcome.

When asked in August 2003 about what kind of political system Sistani saw as being fit for Iraq, Sistani responded: "A system that adopts the principle of consultation, pluralism, and respect for the rights of all citizens."[19] The consultation, or *shura*, referred to here is a mechanism to discover the will of the majority, a key part of representative democracy. Sistani believes elections and parliamentary democracy are the most suitable methods of government for Iraq.

Sistani's many statements and positions in the 2005–20 period show that he wants a vibrant parliament chosen through elections, which produces an inclusive but majoritarian government that is strong and capable of enforcing the rule of law. Several times, he warned of autocratic tendencies and called on parliament to fulfill its responsibilities in creating the right legislation and holding the executive to account. He also advised Iraqis many times to choose the most suitable representatives in parliament based on their capabilities and integrity. Sistani's approach is born out of a "sincere belief in the political legitimacy of a social contract between rulers and ruled."[20]

Sistani's iradat al-umma gives people the freedom to make their own choices, but also to accept responsibility for those choices. The will of the people is predicated on constitutionalism and free expression of majority will through elections. Once people have agreed on a constitution and chosen a parliament that legislates and elects a government, people are bound to follow the process or change it as they see fit within those confines. That is why Sistani sees his role as being not to interfere but to guide, so that people make suitable choices—or, if they make poor choices, they must rectify the outcomes by themselves. This perspective of Sistani's is evident in his statements, when he supports the right to protest and calls on the political elite to listen to people's demands.

Interestingly, Sistani has never used the terms "democracy" and "secular" or "civil state," as they do not conform to the language and tradition of Shia jurisprudence, though democracy and civil rights are mentioned prominently in the constitution which Sistani supported. As noted in earlier sections, Sistani is a strong proponent of equality for Iraqis and civil rights, and for the protection and inclusion of ethnic and religious minorities. The Iraqi constitution reflects these ideals, but they are not effectively practiced, which is why Sistani has chided the political elite.

However, Sistani's views on these matters do not mean that he is a liberal and supports maximal freedoms that are not in line with Islamic values. It might be worth considering that Sistani proposes a distinct politics that is neither about liberal democracy nor secularity, nor a post-liberal and post-secular democracy. However, there is not enough evidence available to further explore this type of speculation.

As for the role of Islam, Sistani does not advocate for an Islamic political system, but rather for a government that respects Islamic principles and values, which usually means a government that does not violate Islamic law. As long as there is no contravention of Islam, the marja needs only to guide and advise. This stance can also be considered a form of veto power on the political process, in which the marja intervenes only if Islam is being violated. This condition is based on the reality of Iraq, a Muslim-majority country, and it is unknown what Sistani's view would be if Iraq was not so. However, at several moments, Sistani has resisted increasing Islamization or introducing sharia laws and practices. For example, the sharia courts established by the Sadrists in Najaf in 2004 were disbanded by Sistani after he retook control of the Imam Ali Shrine, and he was critical of the Jafari personal status law proposed in 2014 and 2017 as "violating the rights of all components of the Iraqi people" because it would treat Shia Iraqis differently from other Iraqis and contravene several laws and conventions. Sistani opposed this law despite it being more in line with Shia jurisprudence than the existing personal status law.[21]

Sistani has also expressed his views on some other political issues, such as the territorial integrity and unity of Iraq in relation to attempts at secession by the Kurdistan region, the electoral laws, government programs and cabinet decisions, several pieces of proposed legislation, and foreign state actions in Iraq. However, on many other political and governance issues—such as federalism, decentralization, the management of the economy, and foreign policy—Sistani has not made his views public. His silence on these matters is consistent with his approach of not becoming too involved in the political process and ensuring that both the people and the political elite take responsibility for their choices and actions.

In summary, Sistani's "will of the people" is a vision for an Iraq that is a civil state bound by a constitution and laws that underpin representative parliamentary democracy, but a state that also respects the principles and values of Islam, as chosen by the people themselves. It promotes democratic principles and the democratic process on condition that they do not contravene Islamic values. It does not call for secularism *or* for an Islamic government or a theocracy. Sistani's view is that, as the people make their choices freely, they are bound by them, and it is not for the marja to give or take away any authority from them or take on any responsibility for their choices or in the state.

The Differing View of Wilayat al-Faqih

As discussed above, Sistani's general political ideology is unclear, but his views on wilayat al-faqih are better known. In broad strokes, there is a divide between two views on the political authority of the marja, with Sistani's school—Najaf—believing in a more limited scope of clerical authority, and the other school, that of wilayat al-faqih, believing in a broader scope. This distinction is critical in understanding Sistani's perspective on the application of religious authority: Najaf believes in being practical and prioritizing context, while Tehran believes in pursuing the theory of divine authority to achieve political outcomes.[22]

Sistani's belief in a more limited scope of clerical authority also helps explain why he has not expounded his own political ideology in the way, say, Muhammad Baqir al-Sadr or Ruhollah Khomeini have: Sistani does not believe clerics need to have political ideologies or try to explain or apply them in every circumstance. He has even demurred about differences in perspective within the Najaf school. In some of his comments during private meetings and his classes, Sistani has made it clear that he disagrees with his teacher, Khoei, on several issues, but had often "abstained from mentioning these disagreements in public, as required by the social conventions prevalent among seminarians."[23] Sistani's silence on such disagreements extends to his view of wilayat al-faqih, whereby Khoei is more restrictive and Sistani is more extensive, but both within the confines of the school of Najaf.[24]

Still, it is possible to infer—from his speeches, the work of his students, and other materials—some specifics about Sistani's views on religious authority. Sistani does not subscribe to *wilayat al-faiqh al-'amma* (general guardianship of the jurist) or *wilayat al-faqih al-mutlaqa* (absolute guardianship of the jurist), which he believes is reserved for the Prophet Mohammed and the twelve Imams, but he does adhere to *wilayat al-faqih al-khasa* (specific guardianship of the jurist) or *wilayat al-faqih fi al-umur al-'amma* (guardianship of the jurist over public affairs). In the absolute guardianship model, the faqih or marja has the general authority over people and their wealth and in even those affairs that are not considered essential for rule and order, meaning a wide scope of authority. This wider scope of authority is Khomeini's view, and the current ideology underpinning the political system in Iran. In the other form of guardianship, which Sistani observes, the marja takes on responsibility for public affairs, when he is "elected" by the other maraji, solely in matters of rule and order.[25] In August 2010, however, Sistani added a conditional clause: if a jurist wants to possess guardianship or authority in the state's administration, he must secure the people's general approval (*maqbuliyya 'amma*).[26]

Sistani's differing view of wilayat al-faqih and his rivalry with Iran's system of Islamic republic is partly due to the theoretical underpinnings described above. But it is also a result of the reach and practices of the institution of Iran's supreme leader. Not only is Sistani adamant that Iraq's context is not suitable for an Islamic government—he also does not want Iran's Islamic government to encroach on Iraq or attempt to encourage a similar system to develop. In fact, Sistani has even described himself as a safeguard against the emergence of an Iran-style theocracy in Iraq: "As long as I am alive, the Iranian experience will not be repeated in Iraq," he said in 2004.[27]

While Sistani is careful not to publicly criticize Iran's system or comment on Iranian political affairs (even though he is an Iranian citizen), clerics from the hawza of Najaf are clear that it does not support the Iranian model.[28] This gives Tehran a particular problem for two main reasons: The first is that there is a marja who is senior to Khamenei who has more followers and even more transnational influence, who can limit Khamenei's authority outside Iran. The second is that Sistani can affect the views of Iranian citizens, who can now clearly see an alternate model for the role of a marja in an Islamic society—a guide and not a ruler, and one who seems to be more successful and accepted by the people. This second point is one reason why Sistani has many followers inside Iran, and why the school of Najaf remains the more appealing model to so many Shia Muslims in Iran and elsewhere.

This rivalry has invited a reaction from Iran, which is why it has worked to influence Najaf and sees possibilities to expand its position there after Sistani's death.[29] Khamenei has maintained an office in Najaf since 2004, and his current representative in Iraq, Mujtaba Hussaini, has overseen a campaign to recruit more students into Iran-aligned schools, giving much larger stipends to students than the Najaf hawza.[30] A few years ago, Iran attempted to place Mahmud Hashemi Shahrudi, the former head of the Iranian judiciary and a confidante of Khamenei, as a marja in Najaf who recognized Khamenei's authority.[31] Iran has supported multiple religious leaders, groups, and movements in Iraq since 2003 who have, in return, attempted to undermine Sistani's authority and influence.[32] Recently, Kazem al-Haeri, an Iraqi marja resident in Qom, asked the Shia to submit to Khamenei's authority.[33] These moves and many others are tactical attempts to reaffirm the authority of the Iranian supreme leader in Iraq and other countries, as part of the powers of the guardian jurist.

However, Iranian officials have also been careful to appear publicly respectful of Sistani—including Khamenei himself on several occasions, heads of government and ministers, and key officials. This show of respect signals their realization that Sistani's authority and position is almost impossible to challenge.[34] The more crucial strategic period for Iran will be after Sistani's death, at which point Tehran may be able to exert more influence and perhaps shape the emergence of the next maraji.

But Sistani has already taken steps to mitigate such an attempt. First, he has increased the numbers of students and teachers in the hawza of Najaf and the rise in prestige of classes at schools there by investing in hawza facilities, stipends, and so on. Second, control of the shrines and a massive increase in their activities, finances, and capabilities makes Iraq more of a natural capital for the world's Shia. Third, the Shia Endowment Law makes specific reference to the supreme marja in Najaf, which negates potential for religious authority from Iran. And the law states that the shrines fall under the control of Najaf, which makes it impossible for maraji in Iran to control them, and thus limits their potential role in Iraq.

Despite all this competition and disagreement on the scope of religious authority, it is still easy to overstate the rivalry between Sistani and Khamenei, or that between Najaf and Tehran. There are many points of agreement on religious affairs, politics, and other matters. The relationships between the maraji in Iraq and Iran are extensive, and the networks are overlapping and mostly coopera- tive.[35] Iran has publicly praised Sistani's leadership in Iraq, knowing that, without him, Shia power—and by extension the potential for Iranian influence—would have been far weaker.

And as far as there is a rivalry, Najaf is in a strong position. The holy city's model for clerical authority and its leadership have endured more than a thousand years of tests. More likely than not, Najaf will continue to thrive in the coming years. In contrast, the model of Islamic government in Iran has linked the authority of a marja to the political fortunes of the state and thus is more likely to face severe challenges in the future.

4
Sistani's Legacy

Undoubtedly, Sistani's legacy is his marja'iyya, which encompasses his leadership, interventions, and guidance. Sistani may not have the same scholarly legacy that his teacher Ayatollah Abu al-Qasim al-Khoei has—in terms of teaching and publications. But Sistani's standing as a marja, as this book has shown, is unrivaled in history. The way Sistani has conducted himself, the respect, prestige, power, and influence he built for the marja'iyya, and the positions he has taken during precarious times in Iraq will leave a legacy for all future maraji to look up to.

Indeed, Sistani has created a paradigm for what a marja should be. The six main features of this paradigm are (1) avoiding formal involvement in politics; (2) ensuring the Iraqi people's sovereignty is paramount and that their wishes are freely expressed; (3) offering guidance to politicians but not allying with any of them; (4) maintaining the power and prestige of the marja'iyya by exerting control over the shrines and the hawza and not intervening in every public issue; (5) acting as a leader for all Iraqis and in all their interests regardless of religion or ethnicity; and (6) only intervening in politics when the "structure of society" is under threat or to tackle the most serious issue the state faces

For Shia Muslim communities, Sistani is a source of pride. He renews their faith in religious leadership and shows that it is possible to hold religious, ethnic, national, and other identities concurrently in the modern world. In Iraq, his defense of constitutional democracy and vital political interventions has allowed a state to be established, though Sistani pushes for progressive reforms. For Iraqis, Sistani provided moral leadership during difficult times and, in the words of writer Hassan Abbas, "helped Iraq cope with the trauma of the Saddam Hussein era and then survive the jihadist brutality after 2003 and the Islamic State's reign of terror."[1] What might be called the Sistani paradigm shows how a marja should carry out his obligations in a diverse nation-state and in a manner that promotes respect for freedoms, equality, rights, and sovereignty.

Everyone who has met Sistani in person and conversed with him has come away impressed with his knowledge, insights, and wisdom, and charmed by his warm and welcoming demeanor. He has endured much to protect his integrity, which is why he is widely viewed as "holy, credible and powerful," in the words of *The New York Times*.[2] Those who have assessed his role believe he has been central to preventing Iraq from completely collapsing into all-out chaos or civil war. His interventions in Iraq have led prominent commentators to call for him to receive the Noble Peace Prize.[3] Although Sistani actively tries to limit their influence in Iraq, both the United States and Iran are glad he is there, because of the stability he provides, and worry about what will happen after he is gone.[4]

Answering Critics

The major criticisms of Sistani since 2003 have focused on three topics: his role in politics in Iraq, his hegemony of the marja'iyya, and his tendency toward reclusion.

First, on his role in politics, some Sunni, Kurdish, and secular Iraqi politicians believe that he has unfairly used his influence to secure Shia Islamist primacy at crucial times.[5] They have variously criticized Sistani's backing for the United Iraqi Alliance in 2005, support for several prime ministers, the 2014 fatwa that led to the creation of the PMU, and general support for promoting conservative Islam in the state, including the constitution and in legislation.

Reformists and civil activists also see Sistani as a protector of the current political system who should have done more to support reform efforts, particularly in response to the October 2019 protests.

Critics of Sistani's political role also claim that Sistani helped create the current political system in Iraq, and yet has been unable to force it to reform. In this view, he bears some responsibility for Iraq's precarious situation. And in Najaf, while Sistani is widely respected and supported, some clerics discreetly question whether he was too involved in politics, while others pose the opposite question of whether he was not involved or decisive enough. Even some senior Shia politicians who benefited from Sistani's role believe he has become too involved in politics and should focus on religious issues.[6]

The second type of criticism, regarding Sistani's hegemony over the marja'iyya, focuses particularly on his control of the shrines. This control has led to the marginalization of the other maraji, and has made Sistani by far the most powerful marja of his time, and perhaps ever. This power, combined with the lion's share of followers in the Shia world, is unprecedented. Sistani's supremacy as marja has placed him, for some time, at a higher level than any past version of the primus-inter-pares supreme marja. Some consider this to have created an imbalance in the marja'iyya and concentrated too much power in Sistani's hands and that of his network.[7] The fear is that the concentration of power and resources could destabilize the marja'iyya as an institution and will make the transition harder after Sistani dies, as multiple maraji compete for his position. There is also a concern that Sistani's power has squeezed out the space for criticism, dissent, differing opinions, and objective evaluation of the marja'iyya's performance.

The third type of criticism of Sistani focuses on the fact that he has not been a public figure or provided the kind of public-facing religious leadership that his predecessors did. The expectations were that Sistani would lead prayers in person, teach large classes of students, visit communities, deliver speeches on important occasions, and be more accessible to Shia Muslims. Instead, Sistani has delegated these tasks, partly because he is not comfortable appearing and speaking in public, but also so that the marja'iyya looks more institutionalized.

His secluded approach may have been warranted during Saddam Hussein's regime, but some critics feel the more available attitude of the other great maraji is what is needed in the present time. Sistani's general absence from the social life of the hawza, such as important religious commemorations, and significant events such as the funerals of maraji and senior clerics, can give the feeling that he does not care much for those types of relationships. Sistani does not make any effort to address these criticisms. But it is notable that his son, Muhammad Ridha, has been much more socially active in the past few years.

This criticism may not have much effect on Sistani's legacy, but being aware of such views is important to give his marja'iyya context and to note that not all Iraqis are enraptured followers of Sistani or agree with his actions.

Personal Asceticism

One aspect of Sistani's legacy that deserves more attention is his personal asceticism, which has shielded him from criticism that has plagued other clerics, particularly those involved in politics. Sistani still wears the same clothes from decades earlier, he does not own any property, and he gives away all the gifts he receives.[8] For most of his life, he would receive guests at his home sitting on the ground, only adopting chairs when his advanced age required a change. His home is still very lightly furnished. At several times, Sistani has asked for those who were prosecuted for insulting him, under Iraqi libel and defamation laws, to be released by the Iraqi judiciary, as he has forgiven them. He also prizes humility, and has requested several establishments such as schools to change their names after being renamed in his honor.[9] Once, when he pushed the governor of Najaf to improve security in the city, Sistani told him to begin with searching his own home for weapons before moving onto others. He has never asked the Iraqi government for anything for himself and requires his family and his network to observe all the laws and regulations, despite the fact that the state is willing to forego some of them due to his status. Sistani has not published his own works and many times has asked for people and institutions not to use his photos or promote him.

When Sistani traveled to London in August 2004 for medical treatment, it gave more people an opportunity to observe his behavior and conduct up close.[10] The cleric refused to sleep in a four-poster bed on his arrival in a luxurious apartment in central London, as he was unaccustomed to it, and instead laid his robes on the ground and slept there.[11] He gave his time to every delegation and visitor who made a request to see him, despite his hospital stays. Once, when a mix-up led to his special home-cooked dinner not arriving the night before his heart surgery in a West London hospital, Sistani opened a bag he had brought with him from Najaf which included some dry pieces of bread, and ate that instead. When he overheard news from Najaf that his son was discussing with others and was told of the death toll from Muqtada al-Sadr's Mahdi Army, he wept and said of the fallen, "These are my sons." Sistani refused police protection and UK government support during his stay, and declined an offer from the emir of Kuwait, Jaber al-Ahmad al-Sabah, who was also in London for medical treatment, to pay for his hospital costs.

The fact that Sistani has maintained his ascetic lifestyle despite the immense power and resources he controls has endeared him to Iraqis and foreigners. This reinforces people's trust in him and readiness to heed his words, which allows Sistani to command a universal respect that almost no one else can. The public admiration for Sistani's austere way of life stands in contrast to the widespread loathing for the lavish and excessive conduct of politicians in Iraq, including clerics, whose names will forever be associated with corruption.

Sistani's Sons

Sistani's legacy extends to his family, particularly through his sons Muhammad Ridha and Muhammad Baqir, who are highly regarded in Najaf.[12] Both are mujtahids and teachers of the most advanced stage of study in the hawza (known as the bahth al-kharij). Both also follow closely in their father's path and have adopted his asceticism. Muhammad Ridha, a student of Khoei, Ali al-Beheshti and Murtadha al-Burujerdi, has taught bahth al-kharij publicly since September 2003, and has classes that attract large numbers of students, with several of them publishing reports based on those classes. The reports show the high level of skill and scholarship that Muhammad Ridha possesses, which has earned him much praise and recognition. His ten-volume work of jurisprudence on the hajj is the largest such contribution in Shia Islamic sciences, and there are now dozens of senior teachers in the Najaf hawza who have graduated from his classes. Balancing a strong career in the hawza while also managing his father's office and dealing with all the pressures and time demands that such a role dictates reflects well on his abilities.

Muhammad Ridha's role in politics is well known. He delivers his father's instructions, writes the Friday prayer speeches as dictated, meets with politicians and intermediaries, receives and delivers messages for his father, keeps up to date with information and events, and manages his office and network. While some critics believe that Muhammad Ridha acts independently of his father and does not always keep him informed, I haven't found this to be true, and neither have other senior clerics in the hawza who are familiar with Sistani.[13] Every statement and comment issued in Sistani's name is reviewed by Sistani himself, and Muhammad Ridha follows his father's approach to public engagement as he himself noted in response to a series of questions in February 2004: "The office of His Eminence Sayed [Ali al-Sistani] does not deal with the media except within the limits of necessity, according to the approach that His Eminence laid out for it."[14]

Muhammad Ridha also reads everything published about his father, even articles in foreign languages, and uses the daily evening *barrani* (open forum) at his house to collect information, discuss strategies, and deliver messages. According to those who have interacted with him at length, he is extremely intelligent, and his primary concern is with protecting his father and his legacy. Though his character has softened with time and he has become more approachable, he remains a sharp, vigilant, and careful man who keeps a very close eye on politics, Najaf and the marja'iyya.

Muhammad Ridha's role in his father's marja'iyya changed dramatically after 2003. The Sistani network in Iraq had been severely restricted and the marja'iyya was mostly organized outside Iraq by Sistani's son-in-law and general representative, Jawad Shahrestani, but regime change returned power to Sistani's office in Najaf. Muhammad Ridha took the opportunity to organize the office and expand its network inside Iraq, formalize relationships with representatives and accredited clerics with the office, set up institutions under the auspices of the marja'iyya, and ensure nobody outside the office spoke in Sistani's name. His role in management of the hawza and the shrines is highly centralized and directly governed through the Office of al-Sayed al-Sistani, his father's formal representation, which Muhammad Ridha heads.[15]

Muhammad Ridha also supervises the clerical organization that manages the imams of the mosques and collects religious dues, called al-Mortada Foundation for Culture and Guidance, and another that trains preachers, the Foundation for Religious Instruction and

Guidance; both of these networks were set up by Sistani's office in 2004. These are two of the most important institutions for controlling the Sistani marja'iyya and network. Both of these institutions, along with many others, are run by Muhammad Ridha's students, his associates, and his inner circle.[16] Since 2020, Muhammad Ridha has steadily increased his public interactions, compensating for his father's reduced profile, and also indicating a willingness to assume more public leadership.[17]

Muhammad Baqir, the younger son, is a popular teacher and has authored several books on Islamic sciences. His focus on teaching means that he has left the running of his father's office to his older brother. Some of his students described him to me as a deeply religious and spiritual person who reflects the effort Sistani imparted in the upbringing of his children. Muhammad Baqir's approach is similar to his father's in that he avoids public gatherings and is immersed in research. As he does not have the pressures of public engagement that his older brother faces, Muhammad Baqir is able to travel more easily, meet with people on his father's behalf, and discharge some religious duties and social obligations that ease the burden on his father and brother.

Muhammad Ridha's sons, Hassan (b. 1987), Hussain (b. 1991), Muhsin (b. 2000), and Muhammad Baqir's sons Ahmad (b. 1994) and Jafar (b. 1998), are also clerics and have reached the advanced stages of hawza studies. All five are held in esteem by their teachers and are themselves teachers in the hawza. Hassan is considered a potential future mujtahid, and his eldest son, a teenager, has begun seminary training and will also become a cleric in the near future. Some of Sistani's other grandsons from his daughters are also clerics, and one of his granddaughters is married to a grandson of Khomeini who moved to Najaf in 2018 to advance his hawza training. Through his sons and grandsons Sistani's name will live on and it may be that they also have an important role to play in the future of the marja'iyya.

The Marja'iyya after Sistani

There are understandable concerns and questions about the post-Sistani future in Iraq. These concerns vary from those about who, if anyone, will become the supreme marja, to what the next marja's attitude toward politics will be, to how the marja'iyya will evolve for the remainder of the twenty-first century. In August 2023, Sistani turned ninety-three years old, surpassing the age of his mentor, Khoei, and having the longest major marja'iyya in contemporary history. His impact on the position and institution of the marja'iyya as an institution is so profound that it is difficult to imagine a successor rivaling his influence. His interventions in Iraqi politics have steadied the ship so often that one must wonder how bad things would have gotten without him. Therefore, thinking about the period after his passing makes people nervous.

When Sistani does pass away, it will be one of the most significant events in modern Iraqi history. His death will mark the end of a chapter in post-2003 Iraq, the passing of a figure who helped form the state as it is today and who raised the prestige of Shia Muslims across the world. Millions of Iraqis will take to the streets to join the mourning procession, and the Iraqi state will undoubtedly afford him various types of official recognition. Foreign governments and international organizations will also convey their condolences, since they see Sistani as the man who kept Iraq together after 2003. Sistani will be buried in the Shrine of Imam Ali, where his teachers Khoei and Hussain al-Hilli are buried, as well as some of his ancestors, such as Mir Damad and Muhaqqiq Karaki (famous jurists of the Safavid era). Sistani's death will mark the departure of a giant of Iraqi history, and will be the end of an important chapter in Iraqi and Shia history. He will enter the record of maraji with legendary status.

While some argue that Sistani will be the last marja of his type, in terms of his role and power, he will certainly not be the last marja.[18] Sistani's successors may not wield the same political influence that he has or be as involved in politics, but they will be maraji with significant authority over Shia Muslims in Iraq and the wider world, the religious institutions in Iraq, and the hawza of Najaf. Ever since the time of Imam Muhammad al-Baqir (d. 733), the Shia have had clerics with religious authority, and since Shaykh al-Tusi's arrival in Najaf in 1056, the city has produced maraji who have had influence on Iraq and beyond.[19] The revival of the city's hawza since 2003, and the return of several elite teachers, has ensured that candidates for the marja'iyya will emerge from Najaf.

The question of whether the marja'iyya could move to Qom is moot—it will remain in Najaf, even though, after Sistani dies, there may be more senior maraji in Iran than in Najaf.[20] There are three main reasons why the marja'iyya will not move to Qom. First, Najaf has historically been the seat of Shia clerical authority for the majority of history, even when it comes to affairs in Iran, such as the Constitutional Revolution in the first decade of the twentieth century. Second, the hawza of Qom generally favors Najaf's clerical authority over the Iranian state's wilayat al-faqih. Third, even if no supreme marja'iyya appears in Najaf, clerical authority over Iraq's Shia cannot emanate from Iran, especially when it comes to political affairs and the management of shrines and the hawza.[21]

The Najaf hawza is also in very good health. It has around 20,000 students today with more than 100 mujtahids, of whom at least 70 teach the highest stage of jurisprudence (bahth al-kharij).[22] And there are only two other maraji universally recognized besides Sistani: Ayatollah Muhammad Ishaq al-Fayyadh (b. 1930) and Ayatollah Bashir Hussain al-Najafi (b. 1942). Several others make a claim to be maraji and may even have a small following, but their marja'iyya is not widely recognized in Najaf.[23] It may be that Sistani's son Muhammad Ridha is the most qualified to succeed his father, but the Najaf hawza informally prohibits transfer of the marja'iyya from father to son.[24] For this reason, Sistani's sons, and those of other maraji, including Riyadh al-Hakim and Ali al-Sabzawari, are also disqualified, even though they might otherwise have the stature and credentials.

There is no clearly defined choice yet for a successor to Sistani. The choice will partly depend on when Sistani dies, and who else from the other senior maraji in Najaf are still alive. The commonly accepted criterium is that Shia Muslims should follow the most knowledgeable marja, and after Sistani there is no unanimous choice. Fayyadh is one possible successor, though he is the same age as Sistani, so even if chosen, he might not hold the position for long. Indeed, when considering what happened when Khoei passed, it is likely that a similar generational change will occur, where the next line of maraji will be from a generation younger than Sistani's. A few years of no recognized supreme marja—it is not strictly necessary for there to be a supreme marja—would not be unusual or unexpected. Or, it could also mean a period of short-lived maraji before the generational transfer. This period of transition is what concerns some observers, since it may be a time of weakness for Najaf, and could invite internal and external pressures on the hawza.

The period after Sistani could also see a resurgence of local maraji and a multiplicity of maraji who each have distinct profiles of followers from the Shia community. Historically, there have been many local maraji who operated simultaneously, each leading in their own area. Globalization may have reduced this phenomenon, but in the absence of a marja who could quickly take Sistani's position as the most widely followed marja, the emergence of multiple local maraji is a likely outcome. There are already maraji who have a sizeable following from certain areas. For example, Fayyadh is the marja for many Afghan Shia, Najafi has a strong following in Pakistan, and in the recent past Ayatollah Muhammad Hussain Fadhlallah (d. 2010) was a marja for many in Lebanon. Communities in the Gulf might follow a Bahraini or Saudi marja.[25] In any case, the fact that Sistani does not have a readily apparent, immediate successor makes the possibility of more local maraji more likely.

From the next generation of potential maraji in Najaf, there are currently two leading contenders. Ayatollah Muhammad Hadi Aal Radhi and Ayatollah Muhammad Baqir al-Irawani (both born in 1949) are widely respected and students of Sistani, two traits that make them strong candidates.[26] Ayatollah Muhammad Jafar al-Hakim (b. 1942) and Ayatollah Hasan al-Jawaheri (b. 1949) are also well regarded, and could well become maraji or lend their support to others in a decisive manner. Whatever the case, it is certain that two factors will determine who is chosen: clerics will be evaluated for adherence to the approach of Sistani to the marja'iyya and the influence of the hawza's top scholars.

Because Sistani's marja'iyya is so distinct, it is difficult to see the next senior maraji in Najaf being of a completely different mold. The next generations of maraji will have to follow in Sistani's footsteps and adopt his approach to the marja'iyya in order to be accepted. Sistani lived through and shaped a transition that dramatically shifted the fate of the Shia in Iraq. Sistani's marja'iyya has created a paradigm for his successors and will be the standard against which they will be judged. They may not behave identically to him, but they will have to act within the confines of that successful model if they wish to become senior maraji in Najaf, and certainly if they want to become the supreme marja. Following the Sistani paradigm will ensure that the candidates for the marja'iyya are able to bear the burdens of the office in the context of the challenges of both Iraq and the wider world. This Sistani legacy will be the most important factor in identifying who the next maraji are, and the adherence to it will be the condition for their acceptance by the Najaf hawza. Some may see this legacy as an impossibly high standard, but Sistani's successors do not need to completely emulate Sistani in their political role. Rather, they should not try to emulate him, and should perhaps adopt a more cautious approach that is more in line with the traditional role of maraji. The Sistani paradigm makes it clear who cannot be a marja but does not burden his successors with political expectations.

The next supreme marja will almost certainly be chosen by senior scholars in Najaf who teach the bahth al-kharij stage, have the largest classes, and exert the most influence among the critical mass of students and followers.[27] It was this group that helped Sistani to the position after Khoei, and for Khoei after Hakim. They will testify which marja they believe to be the most knowledgeable or should be followed and will create momentum for one of the maraji to adopt the position. The most important scholar of this group is Sistani's son, Muhammad Ridha, who could imitate his predecessors Yusuf Al-Hakim (Muhsin al-Hakim's eldest son, who also managed his father's office and directed people to follow Khoei after his father's death) and Muhammad Taqi al-Khoei in directly referring his father's followers to the next supreme marja. Or, Muhammad Ridha could use his substantial influence among the mujtahids and ahl al-khibra (the people of expertise) to build momentum for Sistani's eventual successor.

Sistani himself may yet attempt to clarify who his preferred successor is, but would do so indirectly, as the marja'iyya is not seen as something to be bestowed or inherited.

The Need to Evolve

The marja'iyya has arguably never been in a stronger position, in terms of followers, influence, prosperity, and networks. Control of the shrines and supervision of the Shia Endowment means that Najaf will become stronger in the future, as its resources increase and with a steady growth in student numbers alongside greater prestige and independence from the state gives it an advantage over other hawzas.

But the marja'iyya will have to evolve. The next generation of maraji will have to continue modernizing and be more public and in contact with people than Sistani. That's because there is a significant anti-Islamist backlash in Iraqi politics. Nevertheless, Iraqis are still largely religious and conservative, and the marja'iyya is still respected and relevant. But if the marja'iyya is to retain this status after Sistani's death, it will have to embrace modern tools for connecting with adherents, while also maintaining a distance from politics and contributing positively to society. So far, the marja'iyya has shown that it has this ability to adapt. Projects undertaken by the shrines, particularly those in Karbala, have presented a credible vision of the marja'iyya's role and impact. Even though religiosity and trust in religious leaders has been on the decline in Iraq, the marja'iyya has built a foundation to grow its core following. As more families use the services it provides, such as healthcare and education, they become supporters of its work—in stark contrast to their relationship with politicians, who have been unable to deliver on promises.

Control of Resources

The maraji have used religious dues, mostly *khums* (a 20 percent wealth tax) collected from followers, to fund the hawzas (including stipends for students), build mosques and religious schools, and keep the marja'iyya functioning throughout history. The collection of khums and the management of stipends, endowments, religious shrines, properties, and other wealth are major factors in the marja'iyya's power.

The most senior maraji have been those who tended to have greater control of these resources. Regime change in Iraq in 2003 allowed the marja'iyya, which was almost exclusively Sistani's, to reassert control over the shrines and significant influence on the Shia endowments. The marja'iyya then invested the funds from these institutions in companies and projects, which are now generating hundreds of millions of dollars per year. These revenues dwarf the religious dues collected, which means the marja'iyya is no longer dependent on followers and believers to support them and the hawza. This financial health has allowed the marja'iyya to expand its footprint in Iraq, future-proof income streams, and modernize religious institutions.

The marja'iyya's resources ensure that it will continue to be independent of government and resist being co-opted by internal or external powers. The financial autonomy of the marja'iyya will give it more power and impact in Iraq and abroad. The shrines now manage hospitals, schools, universities, and factories, and are involved in water management, construction, the new Karbala airport, and other sectors in several governorates. More direct delivery of services to the public will further strengthen the marja'iyya's position. In the future, the shrines may expand into other sectors, such as banking, and become a major component of the Iraqi economy.[28]

The Hawza

In the years after regime change that gave space for the Najaf hawza to grow again, one issue that came up was how the status of students in the hawza could change. Would the marja'iyya approve of a plan to increase institutionalization and give the Shia Endowment more say in the affairs of the shrines and the hawza? There was one proposal to increase the stipends of students to levels of public sector employees. Sistani essentially rejected this idea because he was concerned about state co-optation of the hawza and undermining the marja'iyya's independence. Sistani instead insisted that students come to the hawza not looking for employment, and earn the minimum amount that people on social welfare are paid.[29] This remains the situation today, with students earning 125,000 Iraqi dinars a month (around $85) in stipends from Sistani's office.[30]

At the same time, the marja'iyya has completed several projects, such as housing, hospitals, and schools, that offer free or subsidized costs that hawza students are able to access, therefore easing their financial burdens. Thus, even though their stipends are modest, students are assured of access to services, which means they are not dependent on other sources of income, but will also not be drawn to the clergy as a means to financial wealth.

In conclusion, the future of the marja'iyya as an institution looks to be secure, the hawza is healthier than ever before, and there are several credible candidates who could become the maraji of the future. At the same time, the maraji of the future are not expected to wield the same political power and influence that Sistani has.

It is likely that there will never be another marja like Sistani—one who wields much informal power, has a significant influence on politics, yet remains out of public life, in contrast to his predecessors and peers. This ability to impact events, particularly in Iraq, while staying above the fray is what makes Sistani unique. His advocacy for a civil state based on parliamentary democracy, combined with his policy of limited intervention of the marja'iyya, makes Sistani one of the most significant maraji in history. He may well be the last of the greats or, in the words of the scholar Abdullah F. Alrebh, "the last legend, the last transnational grand marj'a recognized by the majority of Shi'a Muslims with the power of fatwa to affect the entire region."[31]

Whatever the future holds for Najaf, Sistani's role as marja is like no other before him, and it is hard to imagine someone playing the same role as him in the near future.

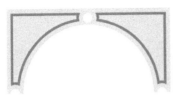

Notes

Introduction

1. See for example Abbas Kadhim, *Reclaiming Iraq: The 1920 Revolution and the Founding of the Modern State* (Austin: University of Texas Press, 2012).

2. Sistani is an Iranian of Arab origin. For much of the history of Shia Islam, non-Arabs and non-Iraqis have been the majority, and therefore it is natural that many maraji and clerics in the Hawza are also non-Iraqi.

3. For example, Mirza Shirazi on state's economic powers, Akhund Khurasani on constitutionalism, Muhsin al-Hakim on communism, Muhammad Baqir al-Sadr on the Ba'ath, Ruhollah Khomeini on Islamic government; see Jawdat K. Al-Qazwini, "The Religious Establishment in Ithna'ashari Shi'ism: A Study in Scholarly and Political Development" (PhD diss., School of Oriental and African Studies, 1997).

4. See Max Weber, *Economy and Society* (Berkeley: University of California Press, 2013, originally published in 1921).

5. See Pierre Bourdieu, "The Forms of Capital," in *Handbook of Theory and Research for the Sociology of Education*, ed. J. Richardson (New York: Greenwood, 1986), 241–58, available at https://www.marxists.org/reference/subject/philosophy/works/fr/bourdieu-forms-capital.htm.

6. Toby Dodge, "Bourdieu Goes to Baghdad; Explaining Hybrid Political Identities in Iraq," *Historical Sociology* 31, no. 1 (2018): 25–38.

7. See James A. Bill and John Alden Williams, *Roman Catholics and Shi'i Muslims: Prayer, Passion, and Politics* (Chapel Hill: University of North Carolina Press, 2002) and Vali Nasr, *The Shia Revival: How Conflicts within Islam Will Shape the Future* (New York: W. W. Norton, 2006).

8. See Abdulaziz Abdulhussein Sachedina, *The Just Ruler in Shi'ite Islam* (New York: Oxford University Press, 1988), Hamid Mavani, *Religious Authority and Political Thought in Twelver Shi'ism* (New York: Routledge, 2013), Mohammad R. Kalantari, *The Clergy and the Modern Middle East* (London: I. B. Tauris, 2022), Ahmad Kazemi Moussavi, "The Struggle for Authority in the Nineteenth Century Shi'ite Community" (PhD diss., McGill University, 1991), Linda S. Walbridge, *The Most Learned of the Shi'a* (New York: Oxford University Press, 2001).

9. Though it could be argued that his statements and rulings (including his online presence) are a form of published expressions of his political views.

10. "Biography," the official website of the Office of His Eminence al-Sayed Ali al-Husseini al-Sistani https://www.sistani.org/english/data/2/.

Chapter 1

1. The majority of Shia Muslims are known as Twelvers or Imamis, as they believe in twelve Imams or leaders after the Prophet Mohammed, and that Imam Mahdi, the Twelfth Imam, has been in concealment for over a millennium, his eventual return preceding the end times. The references to Shia in this work are to the Twelvers.

2. Mavani, *Religious Authority and Political Thought in Twelver Shi'ism*, 139.

3. While the term marja is relatively new, the role of the jurist in Shia Islam is not. In the eighteenth century, the victory of the Usuli school of Shia Islam over the Akhbari school was a key development that preceded the modern marja'iyya. See Robert Gleave, *Scripturalist Islam: The History and Doctrines of the Akhbārī Shī'ī School* (Leiden: Brill, 2007).

4. The first to lay the foundations for this was Sayed Muhammad Mahdi al-Tabatabaei (d. 1798), known as Bahrululoom, who organized and distributed the various leadership positions of the hawza among his students. The first to necessitate following the most knowledgeable mujtahid, and thus to formalize the notion of a supreme marja, was Shaykh Murtadha al-Ansari (d. 1864). See Zackery Mirza Heern, "Thou Shalt Emulate the Most Knowledgeable Living Cleric: Redefinition of Islamic Law and Authority in Usuli Shi'ism," *Journal of Shi'a Islamic Studies* 7, no. 3 (2014): 321–44.

5. al-Qazwini, "The Religious Establishment in Ithna'ashari Shi'ism."

6. Mavani, *Religious Authority and Political Thought in Twelver Shi'ism*, 14.

7. Historically, the death dates for most Shia clerics were recorded and reported accurately, but not their birth dates. Except in the case of living and more recent clerics, this book continues this tradition.

8. Mavani, *Religious Authority and Political Thought in Twelver Shi'ism*, 15.

9. Kalantari, *The Clergy and the Modern Middle East*, 4.

10. The general concept of wilayat al-faqih is also accepted by the Najafi school, they differ on its extent, application and conditions, the term mutlaqa refers to absolute authority, which distinguishes the two views.

11. Similar to the Pope or other orthodox religious figureheads.

12. There were several efforts to exert more control over the hawza, for example the Oudh bequest over which the British took over administration. See Meir Litvak, "A Failed Manipulation: The British, the Oudh Bequest and the ShīʿīʿUlamā' of Najaf and Karbalāʾ," *British Journal of Middle Eastern Studies* 27, no. 1 (2000): 69–89.

13. A mujtahid is an expert cleric who has reached the stage of ijtihad, which means he has mastered the Islamic sciences and is able to deduce jurisprudential rulings from the sources. Mujtahids teach bahth al-kharij, the highest stage in the hawza, which does not rely on a set text and where the teacher gives and defends his decisive opinions on jurisprudence.

14. Sajjad Rizvi, "The Making of a *Marja'*: Sīstānī and Shi'i Religious Authority in the Contemporary Age," *Sociology of Islam* 6, no. 2 (June 2018): 170.

15. A marja opens an office to the public to address its queries and collect religious dues, issue statements, publish works of jurisprudence, use students and clerical networks to distribute stipends, manage endowments and charitable projects, and generally to establish himself.

16. For example, Sistani's two immediate predecessors, Hakim and Khoei, both taught publicly until their deaths, appeared regularly in public and during pilgrimages, opened charitable projects in person, and engaged heavily in the social life of the hawza.

17. Sistani reads all the proceedings from the Iranian parliament and reviews the writings of key thinkers and scholars who have emerged from Iran.

18. Elvire Corboz, "The Najafi Marja'iyya in the Age of Iran's Vali-Ye Faqih (Guardian Jurist): Can It Resist?," Project on Middle East Political Science, http://pomeps.org/the-najafi-marjaiyya-in-the-age-of-irans-vali-ye-faqih-guardian-jurist-can-it-resist.

19. See Kalantari, *The Clergy and the Modern Middle East*; and Mavani, *Religious Authority and Political Thought in Twelver Shi'ism*, for more on Shia religious authority in the Twentieth Century.

Chapter 2

1. The Sistani family is from the Marashi branch of Hussaini Sayeds (family trees are available in libraries in Karbala, Qom, Tehran, and Mashhad). The family's ancestor is Imam Hussain, son of Imam Ali. The line continues through his son Imam Ali Zain al-Abideen, then his son Hussain al-Asghar, who was killed in Madinah and whose descendants then fled Arabia and settled firstly in the Levant and southern Turkey (Kahramanmaraş, thus the name Marashi) and later in northern Iran along the Caspian coast, chiefly Gorgan and Tabaristan, and then Isfahan. The Sistani family is proud of its lineage; between Ali al-Sistani and Imam Hussain are thirty-six ancestors, nearly all of whom are leaders and clerics. The surname Mujtahidi has also been used by the family in recent history, reflecting the mujtahid status of their ancestors.

2. Sistani's grandfather was a highly regarded cleric, being a student of Mirza Shirazi, then Sayed Ismail al-Sadr, and a contemporary of Akhund Khurasani and Mirza Naini, with whom he disagreed on the nature of the Constitutional Movement in Iran, even ending up in prison while in Mashhad due to his critical views. There is an anecdotal story that he predicted his grandson would become a marja. He is buried on the right side of the entrance to the inner sanctum at the Imam Ridha Shrine in Mashhad.

3. There is a story about Sistani's father that came to light after his death, though the Sistani family do not actively promote it. Apparently, Muhammad Baqir al-Sistani performed prayers that enabled him to meet with the hidden Twelfth Imam Mahdi, where the Imam was preparing to pray over and bury a woman who had remained indoors for seven years after the Pahlavi regime banned the hijab. This story may have had an effect on Ali al-Sistani's position during the regime of Saddam Hussein, as noted later.

4. Traditionally, clerical families are very keen on privacy especially when it comes to women in their households, which is why names of female relatives are withheld publicly, including in official biographies.

5. His extended family and relatives are still in Mashhad, though some also reside in Qom.

6. Sistani is the inheritor of his grandfather's works and library, in addition to holding in trust some of the works and memorabilia of Mirza Shirazi through his father-in-law.

7. Abd al-Adhim al-Muhtadi al-Bahrani, *Stories and Recollections of the Ethics of Religious Scholars* (in Arabic), (Beirut: Al-Balagh Foundation, 2009), 418. Isfahani was the founder of the *tafkeeki* (deconstructionist) school in Islamic thought (no relation to Jacques Derrida's school). Sistani recounts in that experience that he learned the importance of humility as a student.

8. For more on his teachers in Mashhad, see the official website of the Office of His Eminence al-Sayed Ali al-Husseini al-Sistani, "Biography."

9. Burujerdi regarded Sistani highly. See Babak Rahimi, "Ayatollah Sistani and the Democratization of Post-Ba'athist Iraq," USIP, 4, https://www.usip. org/sites/default/files/sr187.pdf; and "al-Sayed al-Sistani in the Class of al-Sayed al-Burujerdi—al-Sayed al-Madadi" (in Arabic), uploaded to the YouTube channel Majmuat Al-Sirat (@user-ej3ov2bk4h) on July 25, 2020, https://www.youtube. com/watch?v=o61rJCEX9es. The latter source gives further credence to Sistani being a mujtahid before arriving in Najaf.

10. Burujerdi adopted a methodology that placed more emphasis on the narrations of the Imams for deriving jurisprudential rulings alongside more stringent review of the narrators and the transmission of the narrations. Sistani's jurisprudential methodology is based on Burujerdi's, which generally makes him more of a conservative jurist than his peers.

11. For more on Burujerdi, see Mohammadjavad Ardalan "The Life and Work of a Grand Ayatollah in Historical Context" (PhD diss., St Antony's College, 2013).

12. According to a source, the young Sistani attended Khomeini's lectures in philosophy in Qom for six months and met him regularly when he came to Najaf. See also Ahmad Ali al-Hilli, "al-Sayed al-Sistani and al-Shahid al-Sadr" (in Arabic), April 22, 2021, http://ijtihadnet.net/السيد-السيستاني-دام-ظله-والشهيد-الصدر/.

13. John L. Esposito, *Islam and Politics* (Syracuse: Syracuse University Press, 1998), 128. In 1952, Khomeini suspended relations with Burujerdi until the latter's death in 1961.

14. The modernization and strengthening of the marja'iyya by Burujerdi also informed Sistani's perspective post-2003 with his own marja'iyya.

15. The room he stayed in for a few years is still in use. After getting married, Sistani moved to Kufa and later rented a small house in the Buraq area of the old city in Najaf which is still his home today. It is a seventy square-meter house rented since 1970 from the Shubbar family, which administers the endowment the house is a part of, at a cost of 600,000 Iraqi dinars per month (around $475). See "Find Out the Cost of Renting Sistani's House" (in Arabic) *Sky Press*, 23 April 2016, http://www.skypressiq.net/2016/08/23/تعرف-على-كلفة-ايجار-منزل-السيستاني.

16. Comments to the author, London, 2008. Evidence to back this comes from a letter written in mid-1951 by the prominent Sayed Ali al-Bahbahani to Sistani while he was still in Qom praising his acumen, following a debate by correspondence between them on fiqh issues, see Sistani's official biography on his website.

17. He had a vast appetite for learning and sought out the best teachers on a variety of subjects outside of formal classes, including Sayed Hasan al-Bujnurdi (d. 1975).

18. Sistani built a seminary in Najaf in honor of Hilli. See "Ayatollah Sheikh Hussein al-Hilli School for Religious Sciences—al-Najaf al-Ashraf" (in Arabic), official website of the Office of His Eminence al-Sayed Ali al-Husseini al-Sistani, https://www.sistani.org/arabic/social-service/26485/.

19. Another, in expertise of the Hadith and Rijal sciences, was issued by Agha Buzurg (d. 1970). See Sistani's official biography. Ijtihad licenses are rare because it was never a formal requirement for a mujtahid, though it aids in gaining public recognition and, in the modern era, helps to distinguish mujtahids recognized by the hawza and those who claim to be a mujtahid but are not deemed to be so.

20. It seems Sistani missed the scholarly world of Najaf which outshone the much smaller hawza in Mashhad and was further encouraged to change his mind by one of his teachers, Ayatollah Hakim, who wrote a letter asking him to return to Najaf. See Abd al-Hadi al-Hakim, *al-Najaf al-Ashraf and Its Hawza* (Karbala: Dar Al-Kafil, 2018, in Arabic), vol. 5, 186.

21. See Roy P. Mottahedeh, "The Najaf Ḥawzah Curriculum," *Journal of the Royal Asiatic Society* 26, no. 1-2 (2016): 341–51 for details on the hawza stages.

22. He desired to remain like his teacher Ayatollah Hilli, as some anecdotes quote him saying that he wished not to become a marja and that he could live the simple life and remain dedicated to teaching like Hilli.

23. "Al-Sayed Abu al-Qasim al-Khoei" (in Arabic), Library of the Haydary Shrine, https://www.haydarya.com/?id=149.

24. His classes were in Farsi (after August 1992, in Arabic), attended by small groups of around thirty students, and his teaching style was dense, with some courses lasting well over a decade. Audio recordings of most of his classes are available in Najaf. For a description of Sistani's teaching style see this translated interview with one of his students, Ali Teymoori, "Ayatollah Sistani's Doctrine Differs from Ayatollah Khoei's One," Itjihad Network, September, 26, 2020, http://ijtihadnet.com/ayatollah-sis- tanis-doctrine-differs-ayatollah-khoeis-one.

25. Sistani dislikes fame and has resisted publishing his own works.

26. Hakim, *al-Najaf al-Ashraf*, vol. 5, 188–9.

27. See Abbas Kadhim, "The Hawza under Siege: A Study in the Ba'th Party Archive," Institute for Iraqi Studies at Boston University, Occasional Papers no. 1, June 2013; and Marsin R. Alshamary, "Prophets and Priests: Religious Leaders and Protest in Iraq" (PhD diss., Massachusetts Institute of Technology, 2020).

28. Despite Khoei's position, he was unable to prevent these executions, even though he personally petitioned the regime for the release of senior clerics who were not overtly political, such as Muhammad Taqi al-Jawaheri and Muhammad Taqi al-Jalali.

29. Family members viewed his death suspicious as it occurred shortly after a hospital visit.

30. Early on, Sistani was noted to be immersed in his research and somewhat socially distant. He limited his social interactions in hawza circles, and in his classes, he disagreed with some of Khoei's views, which was rare. However, he clearly possessed important attributes vital for a marja, and his potential to be one was noted early on. See, for example, this prediction by Ayatollah Sadr from the early 1970s. "Martyr Muhammad Baqir Al-Sadr's Outlook on the Future of Sayed al-Sistani" (in Arabic), uploaded to the YouTube channel Ali al-Khalidi (@Alialkhaldi313) on April 11, 2017, https://www.youtube.com/watch?v=E4IL3vu8Ls8.

31. One of Sistani's students related to me a story: in 1987, Khoei had asked Sistani to visit him when a large crowd of clerics and laymen had gathered because the latter was an infrequent visitor to the "*barrani*" and Khoei wished more people became aware of Sistani's stature.

32. Sistani reluctantly accepted after Khoei hinted that he could issue a religious obligation on him. See Sistani's official biography.

33. How a marja assumes the post is a mix of factors. He cannot be appointed or elected in a formal sense, and most will have only a small number of followers see Sajjad Rizvi, "The Making of a *Marja'*."

34. The uprising (Intifadha), which began in Basra after the Iraqi army's defeat and withdrawal from Kuwait, quickly spread to other cities. It began in the month of Shaaban, which is why it is known as the Shaaban Uprising (al-intifadha al-Shaabaniya). This event had a significant impact on Najaf and the Shia of Iraq, the consequences of which are still felt today.

35. "The Shaaban Intifadha" (in Arabic), Library of the Haydary Shrine, https://www.haydarya.com/maktaba_moktasah/21/book_37/01.htm.

36. For more on the 1991 uprising, see "Endless Torment: The 1991 Uprising in Iraq and Its Aftermath," Human Rights Watch, June 1992, https://www.hrw.org/reports/1992/Iraq926.htm.

37. According to a student of Sistani and also noted in the official biography and "The Suffering of al-Sayed al-Sistani and His Two Sons in the Prisons of the Tyrant Saddam Hussein during the 1991 uprising" (in Arabic), published to YouTube to the channel Ibrahim Alhassani (@ibrahimalhassani) on May 19, 2022, https://www.youtube.com/watch?v=iYrhZN5zqZQ.

38. See the archive video, "Funeral of Imam Al-Khoei", uploaded to the YouTube channel Al-Khoei Institute (@Alkhoei_institute) on April 2, 2019, https://www.youtube.com/watch?v=_Tuug-wMwa0. The funeral prayer has a particular significance in hawza circles; Sistani led it in accordance with Khoei's wishes, and this was another signal that he would be Khoei's successor.

39. The regime had correctly deduced that Sistani would be Khoei's successor and that Khoei's son, Muhammad Taqi, and some other scholars from Khoei's inner circle would back Sistani and support his marja'iyya, so the regime began a campaign to target them, assassinating Muhammad Taqi al-Khoei in July 1994.

40. The legacies of the hawza's experiences under the Ba'ath regime and later public attitudes are discussed in Marsin R. Alshamary, "Prophets and Priests."

41. Publishing such a work is one of the prerequisites for a marja to be recognized and followed.

42. Most maraji state that it is compulsory for believers to follow the most knowledgeable jurisprudent in Islamic laws.

43. Organizations such as the Al-Khoei Foundation and the World Federation of Khoja Shia Ithna-Asheri Muslim Communities were instrumental in aiding Sistani's growing reputation, as were the transnational activities of Sistani's network and his offices in Qom, Beirut, Damascus, and London.

44. As his marja'iyya began to establish itself, Sistani appointed new representatives throughout Iraq (rather than retain those from Khoei's, as might have been expected) who became more in touch with the general population than traditional clerical elites.

45. In terms of followers at the turn of the millennium, it was Sistani, Khamenei, Fadhlallah, Shirazi, followed by other maraji with much smaller followings such as Tabrizi, Khurasani, Lankarani, Hakim, and Haeri. Sistani's longevity, a thirty-year-old marja'iyya at the time of writing, has also helped in absorbing followers from other deceased maraji. The majority of Shia Muslims who follow a marja, around 80 percent according to one estimate, now look to Sistani.

46. Since then, Sistani has only left his house a handful of times, such as his visit to London in August 2004 for medical treatment and to visit the other maraji Ayatollah Hakim and Ayatollah Fayyadh in March and August 2011 respectively, and to Karbala for hospital treatment in January 2020.

47. The profound impact of the psychological trauma the Sistani family, as well as the other clerical families such as Hakim, Bahruiloom, Sadr, Khoei, were

subjected to under the Ba'ath regime should not be underestimated. See Abd al-Sahib al-Hakim, *An Encyclopedia on the Killing and Persecution of Religious Authorities, Scholars and Students of the Religious Seminary of the Shia of the Country of Mass Graves Iraq 1968-2003* (Morden: Human Rights in Iraq Organization, 2005, in Arabic).

48. See Abbas Kadhim, "The Hawza under Siege"; Samuel Helfont, *Compulsion in Religion: Saddam Hussein, Islam, and the Roots of Insurgencies in Iraq* (New York: Oxford University Press, 2018); Aaron M. Faust, *The Ba'hification of Iraq: Saddam Hussein's Totalitarianism* (Austin: University of Texas Press, 2015); and Lisa Blaydes, *State of Repression: Iraq under Saddam Hussein* (Princeton: Princeton University Press, 2018).

49. On one visit to Sistani's home in 2003 I was shown the exact spot, right outside the front door, that armed regime security agents would be stationed around the clock, keeping a close eye on all movements and keeping the family in constant concern for their safety.

50. Hamid Al-Khaffaf, *Texts Issued by His Eminence al-Sayed al-Sistani on the Iraqi Issue* (Beirut: Dar Al-Moarikh Al-Arabi, 2009, in Arabic), 94.

51. Ali al-Moimin, "The Shia Hawza Seminary between Najaf and Qom" (in Arabic), *Shafaq News*, August 4, 2021, https://shafaq.com/ar//مقـالات الحوزة-العلمية-الشيعية-بين-النجف-وقم.

52. "Questions of *Maktaba Magazine* / Hussaini Club in Nabatiya" (in Arabic), the official website of the Office of His Eminence al-Sayed Ali al-Husseini al-Sistani, https://www.sistani.org/arabic/archive/247/.

53. The Shia have had maraji, in various forms, since the major occultation of the Twelfth Imam in 941. In the licenses granted by Sistani's teachers there is a chain of twenty-four masters going back to Shaykh Tusi (d. 1067), thus the reference to 1,000 years.

54. See Abbas Kadhim, "The Hawza under Siege," and Samuel Helfont, *Compulsion in Religion.*

55. See Abbas Kadhim, "The Hawza under Siege" on Ali Kashif al-Ghita; and Harith Hasan Al-Qarawee, "The 'Formal' Marja': Shi'i Clerical Authority and the State in Post-2003 Iraq," *British Journal of Middle Eastern Studies* 46, no. 3 (2019): 487 on Ahmad al-Baghdadi.

56. "Reuters Agency Questions" (in Arabic), the official website of the Office of His Eminence al-Sayed Ali al-Husseini al-Sistani, https://www.sistani.org/arabic/archive/232/.

57. See Amatzia Baram, "From Militant Secularism to Islamism: The Iraqi Ba'th Regime 1968–2003," Wilson Center occasional paper, October 2011, https://www.wilsoncenter.org/sites/default/files/media/documents/publication/From%20Militant%20Secularism%20to%20Islamism.pdf; and Samuel Helfont, *Compulsion in Religion* for more on the Faith Campaign.

58. See Abbas Kadhim, "The Hawza under Siege" on the Hakim religious school incident, for example. Sadr gained control over parts of the hawza system with regime approval, leading to the distrust he faced from the other maraji.

59. Qom was particularly hostile to Sadr, who had dispatched his cousin Jafar al-Sadr, son of Ayatollah Muhammad Baqir al-Sadr, in May 1998 to establish his office there.

60. See for example his comments in "The Rare Interview of the Martyr Sayed Muhammad Sadiq al-Sadr" (in Arabic), uploaded to the YouTube channel Ali Irbid (@Aliirbid) on March 23, 2012, https://www.youtube.com/watch?v=poazM InL6PE; and in Adel Rauf, *Marja'iyya of the Field: Muhammad Muhammad Sadiq Al-Sadr, His Change Project and Assassination Facts* (Damascus: Iraqi Center for Media and Studies, 2006).

61. David Siddhartha Patel, *Order Out of Chaos: Islam, Information, and the Rise and Fall of Social Orders in Iraq* (Ithaca: Cornell University Press, 2022), 33.

62. One incident that caused such tension is Sadr's son Mustafa threatening to deport Ayatollah Bashir Hussain al-Najafi after criticizing Sadr, leading to this response from Sistani: "What Happened between Sayed Al-Sadr and Sayed Al-Sistani" (in Arabic), uploaded to the YouTube channel Mohsen Al-Khafaji (@mohsenal-khafaji5529) on April 2, 2020, https://youtu.be/SOsGPJfwxdw.

63. Tensions between Fadhlallah and the maraji continued for fifteen years, ostensibly based on differences of religious views but also due to the nature of competing offices and retinues.

64. Samuel Helfont, *Compulsion in Religion*, 150.

65. Reidar Visser, "Sistani, the United States and Politics in Iraq: From Quietism to Machiavellianism?," Norwegian Institute of International Affairs, NUPI Paper no. 700, March 2006, 9, https://www.files.ethz.ch/isn/27866/700.pdf.

66. Prewar planning was not focused on religious authority, but much more on tribal authority and on social cleavages. Even though U.S. planners recognized a Shia–Sunni divide, they never made the connection to Sistani or even to Sadr. Documents at the National Security Archive show a focus on ethnic groups as being paramount. See "Desert Crossing Seminar (U): After Action Report," U.S. government, June 28–30, 1999, https://nsarchive2.gwu.edu/NSAEBB/NSAEBB207/Desert%20Crossing%20After%20Action%20Report_1999-06-28.pdf; and others linked from the National Security Archive's site "The Iraq War—Part I: The U.S. Prepares for Conflict, 2001," https://nsarchive2.gwu.edu/NSAEBB/NSAEBB326/index.htm.

67. "Iraq's Top Shia Cleric Given 48 Hours to Leave," *Guardian*, April 13, 2003, https://www.theguardian.com/world/2003/apr/13/iraq5.

68. "Reuters Agency Questions about His Eminence's Private Affairs" (in Arabic), the official website of the Office of His Eminence al-Sayed Ali al-Husseini al-Sistani, https://www.sistani.org/arabic/archive/249/.

69. "Questions of the German Magazine *Der Spiegel*" (in Arabic), the official website of the Office of His Eminence al-Sayed Ali al-Husseini al-Sistani, https://www.sistani.org/arabic/archive/248/.

70. See the statements issued by Sistani's office in April–June 2003 collected in Khaffaf, *Texts Issued by His Eminence Al-Sayed Al-Sistani on the Iraqi Issue*.

71. "Questions of *Washington Post* newspaper" (in Arabic), the official website of the Office of His Eminence al-Sayed Ali al-Husseini al-Sistani, https://www.sistani.org/arabic/archive/252/.

72. "Questions about public property, Sunni mosques and other issues" (in Arabic), the official website of the Office of His Eminence al-Sayed Ali al-Husseini al-Sistani, https://www.sistani.org/arabic/archive/305/.

73. For more on clerical views toward the state and politics, see Marsin Alshamary, "Reimagining the Hawza and the State: According to Shi'a Clerics, What Is the Ideal Relationship between Religion and the State?," POMEPS, December 2017, https://pomeps.org/reimagining-the-hawza-and-the-state-according-to-shia-clerics-what-is-the-ideal-relationship-between-religion-and-the-state.

74. Meeting with the author, Baghdad, March 2023.

75. It is possible that Muqtada al-Sadr's new role in Iraq also pushed Sistani to be more active.

76. Partly, this was to understand if he adhered to a form of wilayat al-faqih that would see Iraq become an Islamic republic, something the United States feared in 1991 when it allowed Saddam to crush the Intifadha.

77. "Questions of Associated Press Agency" (in Arabic), the official website of the Office of His Eminence al-Sayed Ali al-Husseini al-Sistani, https://www.sistani.org/arabic/archive/253/; and official website of the Office of His Eminence al-Sayed Ali al-Husseini al-Sistani, "Questions of *Washington Post* newspaper."

78. Khaffaf, *Texts Issued by His Eminence Al-Sayed Al-Sistani on the Iraqi Issue*, 45.

79. Official website of the Office of His Eminence al-Sayed Ali al-Husseini al-Sistani, "Questions of the German magazine *Der Spiegel*."

80. Ibid.

81. "Reuters Agency Questions" (in Arabic), the official website of the Office of His Eminence al-Sayed Ali al-Husseini al-Sistani, https://www.sistani.org/arabic/archive/232/.

82. Official website of the Office of His Eminence al-Sayed Ali al-Husseini al-Sistani, "Questions of Associated Press agency."

83. "A Query on the Project of Writing the Iraqi Constitution" (in Arabic), the official website of the Office of His Eminence al-Sayed Ali al-Husseini al-Sistani, https://www.sistani.org/arabic/archive/273/.

84. Noah Feldman, "The Democratic Fatwa: Islam and Democracy in the Realm of Constitutional Politics," *Oklahoma Law Review* 58, no. 1 (2005), https://digitalcommons.law.ou.edu/cgi/viewcontent.cgi?article=1255&context=olr.

85. Rajiv Chandrasekaran, "How Cleric Trumped U.S. Plan for Iraq," *Washington Post*, November 26, 2003, https://www.washingtonpost.com/archive/politics/2003/11/26/how-cleric-trumped-us-plan-for-iraq/e82c7c68-ff47-4201-8f2c-26ec4a6999e7/.

86. "Statement of the Office of His Eminence on the assassination of Ayatollah Sayed Muhammad Baqir al-Hakim" (in Arabic), the official website of the Office

of His Eminence al-Sayed Ali al-Husseini al-Sistani, https://www.sistani.org/arabic/statement/1466/.

87. *"Washington Post* Questions about the 11/15/2003 Agreement" (in Arabic), the official website of the Office of His Eminence al-Sayed Ali al-Husseini al-Sistani, https://www.sistani.org/arabic/archive/245/.

88. "100,000 Demand Iraqi Elections," *Guardian*, January 19, 2004, https://www.theguardian.com/world/2004/jan/19/iraq.

89. "A Query on the Interim Government Set Up by the United Nations" (in Arabic), the official website of the Office of His Eminence al-Sayed Ali al-Husseini al-Sistani, https://www.sistani.org/arabic/archive/289/.

90. Official website of the Office of His Eminence al-Sayed Ali al-Husseini al-Sistani, "Questions of Associated Press agency."

91. "San Francisco Newspaper Questions" (in Arabic), the official website of the Office of His Eminence al-Sayed Ali al-Husseini al-Sistani, https://www.sistani.org/arabic/archive/233/.

92. Coalition Provisional Authority, Law of Administration for the State of Iraq for the Transitional Period,, March 8, 2004, https://web.archive.org/web/20090423064920/http://www.cpa-iraq.org/government/TAL.html.

93. "A Reply Letter Addressed to Mr. Lakhdar Brahimi, Including the Position on the Law of Administration for Iraq for the Transitional Period" (in Arabic), the official website of the Office of His Eminence al-Sayed Ali al-Husseini al-Sistani, https://www.sistani.org/arabic/statement/1476/.

94. "A Letter to the President of the Un Security Council Warning against Referring to the State Administration Law in International Resolution 1546" (in Arabic), the official website of the Office of His Eminence al-Sayed Ali al-Husseini al-Sistani, https://www.sistani.org/arabic/statement/1479/; and UN Security Council Resolution 1546 (2004), S/RES/1546 (2004), June 8, 2004, http://unscr.com/files/2004/01546.pdf.

95. Yousif Al-Hilli, "The International Community in the Eyes of Ayatollah Al-Sistani," *US-China Law Review* 19, no. 3 (March 2022): 114–24, http://pure-oai.bham.ac.uk/ws/portalfiles/portal/172207502/Paper_by_Yousif.pdf.

96. UN Security Council, Resolution 1483 (2003), S/RES/1583 (2003), May 22, 2003, https://digitallibrary.un.org/record/495555?ln=en.

97. Official website of the Office of His Eminence al-Sayed Ali al-Husseini al-Sistani, "A query on the interim government set up by the United Nations."

98. The crisis of the constitution and post-2003 government has several dark episodes, including attempts to force an agreement from Sistani on the TAL without him seeing a final version, which no doubt increased his mistrust of American intentions. See Andrew Arato, *Constitution Making Under Occupation: The Politics of Imposed Revolution in Iraq* (New York: Columbia University Press, 2009), 113–14.

99. Sistani's office explicitly rejected the formation of militias and told Sadr to give up his weapons. See "Fox News American Network Questions" (in Arabic), the official website of the Office of His Eminence al-Sayed Ali al-Husseini al-Sistani,

https://www.sistani.org/arabic/archive/243/; and " The Text of the Answer of the Office of His Eminence, Grand Ayatollah al-Sayed al-Sistani in Najaf, to the Questions of the *Washington Post* Correspondent in Baghdad" (in Arabic), Imam Ali Foundation, http://najaf.org/arabic/15.

100. "Appointment of New Governor for Najaf," Coalition Provisional Authority, May 6, 2004, https://web.archive.org/web/20040707043558/http://www.iraq-coalition.org/pressreleases/20040508_bremer_zurufi.html.

101. Christine Hauser and Kirk Semple, "U.S. Announces Warrant for Outlaw Iraqi Cleric's Arrest," *New York Times*, April 5, 2004, https://www.nytimes.com/2004/04/05/international/middleeast/us-announces-warrant-for-outlaw-iraqi-clerics.html.

102. Isam Al-Amiri, "Clarifying the Position of Najaf Hawza Scholars on the Movement of Muqtada al-Sadr" (in Arabic), *Alwasat News*, May 28, 2004, http://www.alwasatnews.com/news/393337.html.

103. Daniel Williams and Scott Wilson, "Sistani Demands Exit of Najaf Combatants," *Washington Post*, May 19, 2004, https://www.washingtonpost.com/archive/politics/2004/05/19/sistani-demands-exit-of-najaf-combatants/7d88ccfb-84bf-4992-8d2b-b42023fa6b94/.

104. "Iraqi Cleric Has Heart Surgery in London," *New York Times*, August 14, 2004, https://www.nytimes.com/2004/08/14/world/iraqi-cleric-has-heart-surgery-in-london.html.

105. Hayder al-Khoei, "Ayatollah Sistani and the Battle of Najaf," *Al-Monitor*, September 9, 2013, https://www.al-monitor.com/originals/2013/09/ayatollah-sistani-and-battle-of-najaf.html.

106. The account published by one of Sistani's representatives aims to establish an official narrative that Sistani's departure from Najaf was unconnected to the battle in Najaf. See Hamid Al-Khaffaf, *The Medical Trip of His Eminence al-Sayed al-Sistani and the Najaf Crisis, 1425 AH—2004 AD* (Beirut: Dar Al-Mouarekh Al-Arabi, 2012).

107. "Sistani Leaves Basra for Najaf, Hundreds Join Convoy," uploaded to the YouTube channel AP Archive (@APArchive) on July 21, 2015, https://www.youtube.com/watch?v=AvH4ZswC3pM.

108. Ayatollah Muhammad Saeed al-Hakim was especially critical of Sadr, see for example "Muqtada al-Sadr Is an Ignorant, Spoiled Child" (in Arabic), uploaded to the YouTube channel Al-Kashif (@Al-Kashif) on September 5, 2021, https://www.youtube.com/watch?v=QuQhPrXA_Mw.

109. Among these were questions on whether smuggling goods across the border were allowed, appropriating properties of former Ba'athist officials, and officials acting beyond their authority but in the public interest. See Khaffaf, *Texts issued by His Eminence Al-Sayed Al-Sistani on the Iraqi Issue*.

110. "A Query on Registering Names in the Voter Register" (in Arabic), the official website of the Office of His Eminence al-Sayed Ali al-Husseini al-Sistani, https://www.sistani.org/arabic/archive/287/.

111. Dawa mainly viewed Fadhlallah as their religious guide, SCIRI looked to Khamenei, and the Sadrists to Kadhim al-Haeri.

112. Sistani chose Hadi Aal Radhi to chair the six-member committee that reviewed party nominees to be candidates for the UIA, see Hakim, *Al-Najaf Al-Ashraf and Its Hawza*, vol. 5, 201–2 .

113. Ibid.

114. The subsequent poor performance of the Shia Islamist parties led Sistani to distance himself from them, never again coming close to endorsing them.

115. See "Al-Sistani's Representative Defends List 169: It Includes All Groups and Does Not Monopolize Television" (in Arabic), *Alqabas*, January 17, 2005, https://alqabas.com/article/148897-ع-احتجاجا-التظاهر-يتابعون-الصدر-أنصار; and Safaal Mansoor, "Sistani Openly Backs Shia Bloc," *IWPR*, November 18, 2005, https://iwpr.net/global-voices/sistani-openly-backs-shia-bloc.

116. "Allawi Calls on Shia Maraji to Stay Away from Politics" (in Arabic), Al Jazeera, March 26, 2005, https://www.aljazeera.net/news/arabic/2005/3/26/علاوي-يدعو-المراجع-الشيعية-إلى.

117. Some days, Sistani and his son Muhammad Ridha would work through the night making edits to the text with aides. Comments from a committee drafting member to the author, June 2019.

118. Kalantari, *The Clergy and the Modern Middle East*, 161.

119. See Visser, "Sistani, the United States and Politics in Iraq," 18; and "Sistani, Tabatabaei and Fayyad Are Calling for a Yes Vote on the Iraqi Constitution" (in Arabic), Kuwait News Agency, September 22, 2005, https://www.kuna.net.kw/ArticleDetails.aspx?language=ar&id=1539423.

120. "Ayatollah Sistani's Representative Abd al-Mahdi Karbalaai in a Friday Sermon in Karbalaa, Iraq: Sistani Calls on Iraqis to Vote 'Yes' on Constitution and Amend Problematic Articles Later," MEMRI, October 14, 2005, https://www.memri.org/tv/ayatollah-sistanis-representative-abd-al-mahdi-karbalaai-friday-sermon-karbalaa-iraq-sistani.

121. "Ambiguity and Dissatisfaction to Cost Shia Alliance," *Financial Times*, December 12, 2005, https://www.ft.com/content/d28fc9e2-6b3b-11da-8aee-0000779e2340.

122. "A Query on the Iraqi Elections" (in Arabic), the official website of the Office of His Eminence al-Sayed Ali al-Husseini al-Sistani, https://www.sistani.org/arabic/archive/288/.

123. Visser, "Sistani, the United States and Politics in Iraq," 19–20.

124. "Pressure Mounts for Iraq PM to Resign," CBS News, March 6, 2006, https://www.cbsnews.com/news/pressure-mounts-for-iraq-pm-to-resign/.

125. "Statement of the Office of His Eminence about the Sinful Attack on the Askariyain Imams Shrine" (in Arabic), the official website of the Office of His Eminence al-Sayed Ali al-Husseini al-Sistani, https://www.sistani.org/arabic/statement/1494/. Sistani's request for a meeting with the other three senior maraji in Najaf was an attempt to present a united front in response to the sectarian crisis. See

"Why Did Sayed Al-Sistani Request a Photo with the Maraji in 2006" (in Arabic), uploaded to the YouTube channel Ashura Al-Mariya (@Ashura.network) on September 25, 2022, https://www.youtube.com/watch?v=kbkWvcmJ304.

126. "Statement of the Office of His Eminence on the visit of the Iraqi Prime Minister-designate, Mr. Nouri Al-Maliki, to His Eminence" (in Arabic), the official website of the Office of His Eminence al-Sayed Ali al-Husseini al-Sistani, https://www.sistani.org/arabic/statement/1497/

127. " Statement of His Eminence's Office after the Iraqi Prime Minister Nouri Al-Maliki's Visit to His Eminence" (in Arabic), the official website of the Office of His Eminence al-Sayed Ali al-Husseini al-Sistani, https://www.sistani.org/arabic/statement/1501/.

128. "His Eminence's Message to the Iraqi People about Sectarian Strife" (in Arabic), the official website of the Office of His Eminence al-Sayed Ali al-Husseini al-Sistani, https://www.sistani.org/arabic/statement/1499/.

129. "Statement of His Eminence's Office on the Agreement on the Withdrawal of Foreign Forces from Iraq" (in Arabic), the official website of the Office of His Eminence al-Sayed Ali al-Husseini al-Sistani, https://www.sistani.org/arabic/statement/1507/.

130. Juan Cole, "The Decline of Grand Ayatollah Sistani's Influence in 2006–2007," Die Friedens-Warte 82, no. 2/3 (2007): 67–83.

131. Kalantari, The Clergy and the Modern Middle East, 148.

132. "King Abdullah II of Jordan," NBC News, December 8, 2004, https://www.nbcnews.com/id/wbna6679774#.UcV3GZymV9s.

133. For example, the movement led by Mahmud al-Hassani al-Sarkhi.

134. Ross Colvin, "Iraqi Messianic Cult Denies Involvement in Battle," Reuters, January 30, 2007, https://www.reuters.com/article/us-iraq-cult-idUKCOL04709120070130.

135. Hamza Hendawi, "Iraqi Shiites protest Al-Jazeera's 'insults,'" Associated Press, May 5, 2007, https://www.heraldtribune.com/story/news/2007/05/05/iraqi-shiites-protest-al-jazeeras-insults/28545657007/.

136. "Saudi Cleric Muhammad al-Arifi Vilifies Shiites, Calling Iraqi Ayatollah Sistani 'an Infidel,'" MEMRI, December 11, 2009, https://www.memri.org/tv/saudi-cleric-muhammad-al-arifi-vilifies-shiites-calling-iraqi-ayatollah-sistani-infidel.

137. Qasim al-Kaabi, "Al-Sistani to Iraqi Politicians: Do Not Make Me a Front for Your Work, Rather Bear the Responsibility" (in Arabic), Asharq Al-Awsat, September 15, 2009, https://archive.aawsat.com/details.asp?section=4&issueno=11249&article=536105#.Y6GKcy8Rp9c.

138. Usama Mahdi, "Al-Sistani Confirms His Neutrality among the Political Forces in the Upcoming Elections" (in Arabic), Elaph, June 6, 2008, https://elaph.com/Web/Politics/2008/6/337520.html.

139. See "Statement of His Eminence's Office on the Provincial Elections" (in Arabic), the official website of the Office of His Eminence al-Sayed Ali al-Husseini al-Sistani, https://www.sistani.org/arabic/statement/1509/; and "Statement of His

Eminence's Office on the Upcoming Parliamentary Elections" (in Arabic), the official website of the Office of His Eminence al-Sayed Ali al-Husseini al-Sistani, https://www.sistani.org/arabic/statement/1511/.

140. Comments to the author in March 2004, with similar comments reported by others, see Salah Abd Al-Razzaq, *Al-Sayed Al-Sistani and His Political Role in Iraq* (Beirut: Dar Al-Mahajja Al-Baydha, 2019), 51.

141. See "Al-Sistani Confirms That Iraq Is Not to Be Ruled by a Sectarian or National Majority, but by a Political Majority" (in Arabic), Radio Sawa, May 30, 2009, https://www.radiosawa.com/archive/2009/05/30/-العراق-يؤكد-السيستاني لا-يحكم-بأغلبية-طائفية-قومية-وإنما-بأغلبية-سياسية; Abd Al-Razzaq, *Al-Sayed Al-Sistani and His Political Role in Iraq*, 53; and Salem Mashkour (@smashkour), Twitter status update ("The Marja Sistani: The majority required to rule Iraq is political, not sectarian or national"), April 26, 2018 https://twitter.com/smashkour/status/989494406221848576?s=21&t=nLWcRZLJfqjgCwL7_ydapA.

142. Mohammad Al-Ghazzi "Iraqi Lawmakers Back Sistani's Call for Open List in Coming Polls", Kuwait News Agency, October 5, 2009, https://www.kuna.net.kw/ArticleDetails.aspx?language=en&id=2029768.

143. See Sistani.org, for example, "A Message to Egyptian President Muhammad Hosni Mubarak after His Statements about the Loyalty of the Shia" (in Arabic), the official website of the Office of His Eminence al-Sayed Ali al-Husseini al-Sistani, https://www.sistani.org/arabic/statement/1495/.

144. "Statement by the Official Spokesperson of His Eminence al-Sayed's Office on What Some News Agencies Reported (The Elections)" (in Arabic), the official website of the Office of His Eminence al-Sayed Ali al-Husseini al-Sistani, https://www.sistani.org/arabic/statement/25924/.

145. "Maliki Clings to Run for the Premiership of the New Iraqi Government" (in Arabic), *Deutsche Welle*, May 29, 2010, https://www.dw.com/ar/المالكي-يتمسك-بالترشح-لرئاسة-الحكومة-العراقية-الجديدة/a-5630968.

146. Barbara Slavin, "Obama Sent a Secret Letter to Iraq's Top Shiite Cleric," *Foreign Policy*, August 5, 2010, https://foreignpolicy.com/2010/08/05/obama-sent-a-secret-letter-to-iraqs-top-shiite-cleric/.

147. "Sistani's Representative Calls for a Reduction in the Salaries of MPs" (in Arabic), *Alrai*, December 8, 2007, https://alrai.com/article/250134/عربي20%ودولي/وكيل-السيستاني-يطالب-بخفض-رواتب-النواب.

148. Jack Healy and Michael S. Schmidt, "Demonstrations Turn Violent in Iraq," *New York Times*, February 25, 2011, https://www.nytimes.com/2011/02/26/world/middleeast/26iraq.html.

149. "Statement of the Office of His Eminence Sayed about the Demonstrations on Friday" (in Arabic), the official website of the Office of His Eminence al-Sayed Ali al-Husseini al-Sistani, https://www.sistani.org/arabic/statement/1515/.

150. "Informed Source: Al-Sayed Ali Al-Sistani Refuses to Receive Ibrahim Al-Jaafari Due to His Dissatisfaction with the Behavior of Political Leaders" (in Arabic), *Buratha News*, March 9, 2011, http://burathanews.com/arabic/news/118752.

151. "Iraqi Vice President Adil Abdul-Mahdi Submits His Resignation" (in Arabic), *Albawaba*, May 30, 2011, https://www.albawaba.com/ar//الأخبار-الرئيسية
.نائب-الرئيس-العراقي-عادل-عبد-المهدي-يقدم-استقالته-375933-

152. "A Close Associate of Al-Sistani Stipulates That the Salaries of the Three Presidencies Be Reduced, with the Aim of 'Trimming' the Government" (in Arabic), *Alanba*, July 23, 2011, https://www.alanba.com.kw/ar/arabic-international-news/214350/23-07-2011--بهدف-الثلاث-رواتبالرئاسات-تخفيض-يشترط-السيستاني-مقرب
./ترشيق-الحكومة

153. "The Religious Authority Refuses to Receive Officials" (in Arabic), *Almada*, August 26, 2011, https://almadapaper.net/view.php?cat=51911.

154. For example, in the January 31, 2014, Friday prayer speech Sistani's, representative asked: "Where is Iraq going? In light of this whirlpool of recurring problems and crises, every day the Iraqi citizen wakes to a problem in Iraq and sleeps facing more problems! So that the problems have led to other problems without us finding a horizon for a solution." "Friday speech" (in Arabic), the official website of the Al-Abbas Holy Shrine, January 31, 2014, https://alkafeel.net/inspiredfriday/index.php?id=145&ser=2&lang=ar.

155. Elie Shalhoub, "Sistani Boycotts Politicians, Not the Political Process" (in Arabic), *Al-Akhbar*, March 20, 2012, https://al-akhbar.com/International/67151.

156. For example, Sistani received the head of the UN Mission in Iraq several times and Turkish foreign minister Ahmed Davutoğlu in November 2011, without any accompanying Iraqi officials.

157. "Friday Speech" (in Arabic), the official website of the Al-Abbas Holy Shrine, January 11, 2013, https://alkafeel.net/inspiredfriday/index.php?id=90&ser=1&lang=ar.

158. For example the Friday prayer speech on February 7, 2014 was very critical of parliament's legislation of increased benefits and financial allocations to senior officials and called on the Federal Supreme Court to strike down that article in the pensions law, see "Friday speech" (in Arabic), The official website of the Al-Abbas holy shrine, February 7, 2014, https://alkafeel.net/inspiredfriday/index.php?id=146&ser=2&lang=ar. Interestingly, the statement notes the marja'iyya is expressing the "will of the people" in this matter.

159. Ali Mamouri, "Tensions Mount between Iraqi Government, Najaf," *Al-Monitor*, August 22, 2013, https://www.al-monitor.com/originals/2013/08/iraq-government-tensions-baghdad-najaf.html.

160. "A Query on Urging Citizens to Choose the Most Qualified Candidate in the Elections and That the Religious Authority Is at the Same Distance from Everyone" (in Arabic), the official website of the Office of His Eminence al-Sayed Ali al-Husseini al-Sistani, https://www.sistani.org/arabic/archive/24568/.

161. Ali Mamouri, "Sistani Calls on Iraqi Voters to 'Choose Wisely,'" *Al-Monitor*, April 15, 2014, https://www.al-monitor.com/originals/2014/04/sistani-call-change-iraq-elections-maliki.html.

162. "The Supreme Religious Authority Calls on Citizens to Research the past of the Candidate They Elect, and Stresses Approving the Budget Because It

Is One of the Basic Duties of This Council" (in Arabic), the official website of the Al-Abbas Holy Shrine, April 4, 2014, https://alkafeel.net/inspiredfriday/index.php?id=154&ser=2&lang=ar.

163. A source close to Sistani's office, comments to the author, August 2014.

164. Wael Hashim, "How and Why Did Mr. Nuri Al-Maliki Step Down?" (in Arabic), *Shafaqna*, August 17, 2014, https://ar.shafaqna.com/AR/15375/ا-نوري-السيد-تخى-ولماذا-كيف-شفقنا-خاص/.

165. "The Supreme Religious Authority Affirms That the Fatwa on the Sufficient Obligation to Defend the Homeland Includes All Iraqis, Regardless of Their Sects, Religions and Nationalities" (in Arabic), the official website of the Al-Abbas Holy Shrine, June 20, 2014, https://alkafeel.net/inspiredfriday/index.php?id=165&ser=2&lang=ar.

166. Abd Al-Razzaq, *Al-Sayed Al-Sistani and His Political Role in Iraq*, 134.

167. "Secretary-General's Exchange with Asia Society President Josette Sheeran Following His Speech at the Asia Society," United Nations, June 20, 2014, https://www.un.org/sg/en/content/sg/press-encounter/2014-06-20/secretary-general's-exchange-asia-society-president-josette.

168. " The Supreme Religious Authority: The Parliament's Success in Overcoming Two Important Milestones within an Acceptable Period of Time Is an Important Step within the Framework of the Required Political Movement" (in Arabic), the official website of the Al-Abbas Holy Shrine, July 25, 2014, https://alkafeel.net/inspiredfriday/index.php?id=170&ser=2&lang=ar.

169. Raya Jalabi, "The Power Struggle in Baghdad and Nouri Al-Maliki's Fight for Survival," *Guardian*, August 13, 2014, https://www.theguardian.com/world/2014/aug/13/iraq-abadi-maliki-baghdad-prime-minister-struggle.

170. "Iraq President Asks Abadi to Succeed PM Nouri Maliki," BBC News, August 11, 2014, https://www.bbc.com/news/world-middle-east-28739975.

171. Abd Al-Razzaq, *Al-Sayed Al-Sistani and His Political Role in Iraq*, 136.

172. Tim Arango, "Maliki's Bid to Keep Power in Iraq Seems to Collapse," *New York Times*, August 12, 2014, https://www.nytimes.com/2014/08/13/world/middleeast/maliki-seems-to-back-away-from-using-military-force-to-retain-power.html.

173. "Pressure Mounts on Defiant Maliki to Step Down," Al Arabiya, August 13, 2014, https://english.alarabiya.net/News/middle-east/2014/08/13/Bomb-explodes-near-home-of-Iraq-s-Abadi.

174. "Maliki Says Abadi's Appointment as Iraqi PM 'Has No Value,'" Reuters, August 13, 2014, https://www.reuters.com/article/cnews-us-iraq-crisis-maliki-idCAKBN0GD0QY20140813.

175. Tim Arango, "Maliki Agrees to Relinquish Power in Iraq," *New York Times*, August 14, 2014, https://www.nytimes.com/2014/08/15/world/middleeast/iraq-prime-minister-.html.

176. Loveday Morris, "A Letter from Sistani Turned the Tide against Iraq's Leader," *Washington Post*, August 13, 2014, https://www.washingtonpost.com/world/middle_east/a-letter-from-sistani-turned-the-tide-against-iraqs-leader/2014/08/13/3b3426cf-60ee-4856-ad26-d01a9c6cc9c3_story.html.

177. "U.N.'s Ban Seeks Advice on Iraq Crisis from Top Cleric," Reuters, July 24, 2014, https://www.reuters.com/article/us-iraq-sistani-idUSKBN0FT1MQ20140724.

178. Caroleen Marji Sayej, *Patriotic Ayatollahs: Nationalism in Post-Saddam Iraq* (Ithaca: Cornell University Press, 2018), 83.

179. Iran sent advisors and munitions immediately, but it took other nations nearly two months before they came to Iraq's aid with the U.S.-led Global Coalition to Defeat ISIS.

180. Sistani's rationale and decision-making process were related to me by two separate sources close to Sistani.

181. "What Was Stated in the Friday Sermon of the Representative of the Supreme Religious Authority in Holy Karbala, Shaykh Abd Al-Mahdi Al-Karbalai on (14 Shaban 1435 Ah) Corresponding to (13/6/2014 Ad)" (in Arabic), the official website of the Office of His Eminence al-Sayed Ali al-Husseini al-Sistani, http://www.sistani.org/arabic/archive/24918/.

182. "The Supreme Religious Authority Affirms That the Fatwa on the Sufficient Obligation to Defend the Homeland Includes All Iraqis, Regardless of Their Sects, Religions and Nationalities" (in Arabic), the official website of the Al-Abbas Holy Shrine, June 20, 2014, https://alkafeel.net/inspiredfriday/index.php?id=165&ser=2&lang=ar.

183. See, for example, Thomas Erdbrink, "In Shiite Heartland of Iraq, Volunteers Get Set for a 'Defensive Jihad,'" *New York Times*, June 21, 2014, https://www.nytimes.com/2014/06/22/world/middleeast/in-the-shiite-heartland-of-iraq-volunteers-gird-for-a-defensive-jihad.html.

184. Official website of the Office of His Eminence al-Sayed Ali al-Husseini al-Sistani, "What Was Stated in the Friday Sermon."

185. Ibid

186. Julian Pecquet, "Obama's Anti-IS Envoy: Shiites Saved Iraq," *Al-Monitor*, February 10, 2016, http://www.al-monitor.com/pulse/originals/2016/02/shiite-militants-iraq-islamic-state-obama-envoy-mcgurk.html.

187. "The Supreme Religious Authority Affirms That the Fatwa on the Sufficient Obligation to Defend the Homeland Includes All Iraqis, Regardless of Their Sects, Religions and Nationalities" (in Arabic), the official website of the Al-Abbas Holy Shrine, June 20, 2014, https://alkafeel.net/inspiredfriday/index.php?id=165&ser=2&lang=ar.

188. "Advice and Guidance to the Fighters on the Battlefields," the official website of the Office of His Eminence al-Sayed Ali al-Husseini al-Sistani, http://www.sistani.org/english/archive/25036/.

189. "The Supreme Religious Authority Congratulates the Heroic Fighters for Their Splendid Victories, and Reaffirms the Need to Protect Citizens in the Combat Zones" (in Arabic), the official website of the Al-Abbas Holy Shrine, February 24, 2017, https://alkafeel.net/inspiredfriday/index.php?id=311&ser=2&lang=ar.

190. "A Query on the Continuation of the Sufficient Defense Fatwa until the Complete Victory over the Terrorists" (in Arabic), the official website of the Office

of His Eminence al-Sayed Ali al-Husseini al-Sistani, https://www.sistani.org/arabic/archive/25582/.

191. Hamdi Malik, "Pro-Sistani 'Popular Mobilization Units' Break with Pro-Iran Militias in Iraq," *Al-Monitor*, April 29, 2020, https://www.al-monitor.com/originals/2020/04/iraq-iran-pmu-sistani.html.

192. For more on the fatwas noted here, see Salah Al-Daami, "The Impact of the Jihad Fatwas of the Shia Imami Maraji in Confronting the Colonial Powers" (in Arabic), *Journal of Kufa Studies Center* 2, no. 61 (2021): 327–63.

193. Abbas Kashif Al-Ghita, "Glimpses of the Positions of Najaf Scholars on the Issue of Palestine" (in Arabic), The General Kashif Al-Getaa Foundation, http://www.kashifalgetaa.com/?id=178.

194. For more on authority to clerical invoke jihad, see Mavani, *Religious Authority and Political Thought in Twelver Shiʻism*.

195. Abd Al-Razzaq, *Al-Sayed Al-Sistani and His Political Role in Iraq*, 227.

196. Sistani received Abadi on October 20, 2014 and Speaker Salim al-Jibouri on November 16, 2014.

197. "Masum Praises the Role of Sayed Sistani and Confirms His Advice in Writing the Constitution" (in Arabic), *Shafaqna*, January 3, 2019, https://iraq.shafaqna.com/AR/136294/معصوم-يشيد-بدور-السيد-السيستاني-ويؤكد/.

198. "Iraqis Protest over Power Outages and Poor Services," Al Jazeera, August 3, 2015, https://www.aljazeera.com/news/2015/8/3/iraqis-protest-over-power-outages-and-poor-services.

199. "The Supreme Religious Authority Calls on the Iraqi Government to Do Its Utmost to Fulfill the Legitimate Demands of Citizens through Appropriate Methods, Warning against Underestimating Them and Not Being Indifferent to Their Consequences" (in Arabic), the official website of the Al-Abbas Holy Shrine, July 31, 2015, https://alkafeel.net/inspiredfriday/index.php?id=223&ser=2&lang=ar.

200. "What Is Required of the Prime Minister Is to Be More Daring and Courageous in His Reform Steps and Not to Be Content with Secondary Steps and to Strike with an Iron Fist Anyone Who Tampers with the People's Wealth" (in Arabic), the official website of the Al-Abbas Holy Shrine, August 7, 2015, https://alkafeel.net/inspiredfriday/index.php?id=224&ser=2&lang=ar.

201. Ahmed Rasheed, "Iraq's Abadi Proposes Clear-Out of Top Government Posts," Reuters, August 9, 2015, https://www.reuters.com/article/uk-mideast-crisis-iraq-reform-idUKKCN0QE05K20150809.

202. "The Supreme Religious Authority Calls for the Adoption of the Principle of Competence and Integrity in Assuming Official Positions and Positions Instead of Partisan Quotas" (in Arabic), the official website of the Al-Abbas Holy Shrine, November 6, 2015, https://alkafeel.net/inspiredfriday/index.php?id=237&ser=2&lang=ar.

203. Kirk H. Sowell, "Abadi's Failed Reforms," Carnegie Endowment, November 17, 2015, https://carnegieendowment.org/sada/62004.

204. "The Supreme Religious Authority: The Battle of Reforms That We Are Waging These Days Is a Crucial Battle That Determines Our Future and the Future of Our Country, and We, as a People and Government, Have No Choice but to Win It," (in Arabic), the official website of the Al-Abbas Holy Shrine, August 21, 2015, https://alkafeel.net/inspiredfriday/index.php?id=226&ser=2&lang=ar.

205. "The Supreme Religious Authority Stresses the Need to Support the Iraqi Army and Continue to Build It on National Foundations, and Expresses Regret at the Failure to Achieve Reforms" (in Arabic), the official website of the Al-Abbas Holy Shrine, January 8, 2016, https://alkafeel.net/inspiredfriday/index.php?id=246&ser=2&lang=ar.

206. "The Supreme Religious Authority Calls on Officials and Political Forces to Be Aware of the Size of the Responsibility Placed on Their Shoulders and That the Iraqi People Deserve to Harness All Their Capabilities to Serve Them" (in Arabic), the official website of the Al-Abbas Holy Shrine, January 22, 2016, https://alkafeel.net/inspiredfriday/index.php?id=248&ser=2&lang=ar.

207. "The Supreme Religious Authority Decides to Make the Political Sermon According to the Requirements of Events and Developments in Iraqi Affairs, and Not on a Weekly Basis" (in Arabic), the official website of the Al-Abbas Holy Shrine, February 5, 2016, https://alkafeel.net/inspiredfriday/index.php?id=250&ser=2&lang=ar.

208. Kareem Raheem and Stephen Kalin, "Iraq's Sadr Begins Sit-in inside Green Zone to Push for Reforms," Reuters, March 27, 2016, https://www.reuters.com/article/uk-mideast-crisis-iraq-sadr-idUKKCN0WT0I8.

209. Nizar Hatem, "The Iraqi Crisis Breaks the Silence of Sistani: Beware of Going Too Far" (in Arabic), Al-Qabas, May 5, 2016, https://www.alqabas.com/article/23850-الأزمة-العراقية-تكسر-صمت-السيستاني-حذ.

210. "SRSG Kubiš Meets with His Eminence Grand Ayatollah Ali al-Sistani in Najaf—30 May 2016," uploaded to the YouTube channel UN Iraq (@UN_Iraq) on May 30, 2016, https://www.youtube.com/watch?v=xa44MVZMf_Y.

211. "The Secretary General of the Holy Shrine of Imam Ali Receives the Iraqi Prime Minister and His Accompanying Delegation" (in Arabic), the Holy Alawi Shrine, https://www.imamali.net/index.php?id=316&sid=5419.

212. "The Text of the Second Sermon Delivered by the Representative of the Supreme Religious Authority, His Eminence Sheikh Abd al-Mahdi al-Karbalai on Friday (19 Muharram 1438 AH)" (in Arabic), the official website of the Office of His Eminence al-Sayed Ali al-Husseini al-Sistani, https://www.sistani.org/arabic/archive/25485/.

213. "The Supreme Religious Authority Clarifies Its Position on the Referendum on the Secession of Northern Iraq (Kurdistan)" (in Arabic), the official website of the Al-Abbas Holy Shrine, September 29, 2017, https://alkafeel.net/inspiredfriday/index.php?id=343&ser=2&lang=ar.

214. "The Supreme Religious Authority Considers What Happened in Kirkuk Not a Victory for One Party over Another, but Rather a Victory for All Iraqis" (in

Arabic), the official website of the Al-Abbas Holy Shrine, October 20, 2017, https://alkafeel.net/inspiredfriday/index.php?id=349&ser=2&lang=ar.

215. "Victory Sermon from Holy Karbala" (in Arabic), the official website of the Office of His Eminence al-Sayed Ali al-Husseini al-Sistani, https://www.sistani.org/arabic/statement/25875//.

216. "Statement of the Office of His Eminence on the Parliamentary Elections in Iraq in 2018" (in Arabic), the official website of the Office of His Eminence al-Sayed Ali al-Husseini al-Sistani, https://www.sistani.org/arabic/statement/26025/.

217. "The Supreme Religious Authority: The Current Government Must Strive to Achieve What Can Be Urgently Achieved of the Citizens' Demands, and That the Next Government Should Be Formed on the Right Basis of Effective and Impartial Competencies" (in Arabic), the official website of the Al-Abbas Holy Shrine, July 27, 2018, https://alkafeel.net/inspiredfriday/index.php?id=396&ser=2&lang=ar.

218. "Supreme Marja'iyya: We Do Not Support Those Who Were in Power in Previous Years for the Position of Prime Minister" (in Arabic), the official website of the Office of His Eminence al-Sayed Ali al-Husseini al-Sistani, https://www.sistani.org/arabic/statement/26114/.

219. "Dialogue with the Director of the Office of His Eminence in Lebanon about the Role of Religious Authority in the Religious and Political Scene" (in Arabic), the official website of the Office of His Eminence al-Sayed Ali al-Husseini al-Sistani, https://www.sistani.org/arabic/archive/26342/.

220. Former member of parliament involved in the negotiations, comments to the author, Baghdad, January 2023.

221. For example, the Iranian president and the Lebanese speaker of parliament. See "His Eminence's Reception of the Iranian President, Dr. Hassan al-Rouhani (13/3/2019)" (in Arabic), the official website of the Office of His Eminence al-Sayed Ali al-Husseini al-Sistani, https://www.sistani.org/arabic/archive/26257/; and "His Eminence's Reception of Mr. Nabih Berri, Speaker of the Lebanese Parliament (1/4/2019)" (in Arabic), the official website of the Office of His Eminence al-Sayed Ali al-Husseini al-Sistani, https://www.sistani.org/arabic/archive/26263/.

222. "His Eminence's Reception of the Representative of the Secretary-General of the United Nations in Iraq (29/11/2018)" (in Arabic), the official website of the Office of His Eminence al-Sayed Ali al-Husseini al-Sistani, https://www.sistani.org/arabic/archive/26116/.

223. "His Eminence's Meeting with the Special Representative of the Secretary-General of the United Nations in Iraq (6/2/2019)" (in Arabic), the official website of the Office of His Eminence al-Sayed Ali al-Husseini al-Sistani, https://www.sistani.org/arabic/archive/26231/.

224. "The Text of the Second Sermon Delivered by the Representative of the Supreme Religious Authority, His Eminence Sayed Ahmad al-Safi, on Friday (10 Shawwal 1440 AH) Corresponding to (14/6/2019)" (in Arabic), the official website of the Office of His Eminence al-Sayed Ali al-Husseini al-Sistani, https://www.sistani.org/arabic/archive/26306/.

225. "Al-Karbalai: The Religious Authority Advised, but What the Country Has Reached Was the Result of Widespread Financial and Administrative Corruption in the Various State Facilities and Institutions" (in Arabic), Imam Hussain Holy Shrine, https://imamhussain.org/arabic/21158.

226. "The Text of the Second Sermon Delivered by the Representative of the Supreme Religious Authority, His Eminence Sayed Ahmed al-Safi on Friday (5 Safar 1441 AH) Corresponding to (4/10/2019)" (in Arabic), the official website of the Office of His Eminence al-Sayed Ali al-Husseini al-Sistani, https://www.sistani.org/arabic/archive/26344/.

227. "The Text of the Second Sermon Delivered by the Representative of the Supreme Religious Authority, His Eminence Sheikh Abd al-Mahdi al-Karbalai, on Friday (12 Safar 1441 AH) Corresponding to (10/11/2019)" (in Arabic), the official website of the Office of His Eminence al-Sayed Ali al-Husseini al-Sistani, https://www.sistani.org/arabic/archive/26350/.

228. See the Friday prayer speeches between October 25, 2019 and November 22, 2019.

229. Reflected in his own comments. See for example readouts from the November 2019 meeting with the UNAMI head Hennis-Plasschaert and the March 2021 meeting with Pope Francis.

230. "His Eminence's Reception of the Head of the United Nations Mission in Iraq (11/11/2019)" (in Arabic), the official website of the Office of His Eminence al-Sayed Ali al-Husseini al-Sistani, https://www.sistani.org/arabic/archive/26358/.

231. "The Text of the Second Sermon Delivered by the Representative of the Supreme Religious Authority, His Eminence Sayed Ahmad al-Safi, on Friday (17 Rabi' al-Awwal 1441 AH) Corresponding to (15/11/2019)" (in Arabic), the official website of the Office of His Eminence al-Sayed Ali al-Husseini al-Sistani, https://www.sistani.org/arabic/archive/26359/.

232. "The Text of the Second Sermon Delivered by the Representative of the Supreme Religious Authority, His Eminence Sayed Ahmad al-Safi on Friday (2 Rabi' al-Akhir 1441 AH) Corresponding to (29/11/2019)" (in Arabic), the official website of the Office of His Eminence al-Sayed Ali al-Husseini al-Sistani, https://www.sistani.org/arabic/archive/26361/.

233. Sistani's statements are here: "A Statement by an Official Source in the Office of His Eminence Sayed (May His Shadow Be Long) about the Attack on the Iraqi Forces in the City of Al-Qaim (30/12/2019)" (in Arabic), the official website of the Office of His Eminence al-Sayed Ali al-Husseini al-Sistani, https://www.sistani.org/arabic/archive/26373/; "The Text of the Second Sermon Delivered by the Representative of the Supreme Religious Authority, His Eminence Shaykh Abd Al-Mahdi Al-Karbalai, on Friday (7 Jumada al-Awwal 1441 AH) Corresponding to (3/1/2020)" (in Arabic), the official website of the Office of His Eminence al-Sayed Ali al-Husseini al-Sistani, https://www.sistani.org/arabic/archive/26374/; and "The Text of the Second Sermon Delivered by the Representative of the Supreme Religious Authority, His Eminence Sayed Ahmad Al-Safi, on Friday (14 Jumada al-Awwal 1441 AH) Corresponding to (10/1/2020)" (in Arabic), the official website of

the Office of His Eminence al-Sayed Ali al-Husseini al-Sistani, https://www.sistani.org/arabic/archive/26375/.

234. "Sayed Sistani Offers Condolences to Sayed Khamenei for the Martyrdom of Major General Qassem Soleimani" (in Arabic), *Shafaqna*, January 5, 2021, https://ar.shafaqna.com/AR/204294/السيد-السيستاني-يعزي-بشهادة-اللواء-قا/. His son Muhammad Ridha also participated in the funeral processions of Soleimani and Muhandis in Najaf.

235. "A Statement by an Official Source in the Office of His Eminence (16/1/2020)" (in Arabic), the official website of the Office of His Eminence al-Sayed Ali al-Husseini al-Sistani, https://www.sistani.org/arabic/archive/26376/.

236. "The Text of the Second Sermon Delivered by the Representative of the Supreme Religious Authority, His Eminence Sheikh Abdul-Mahdi al-Karbalai, on Friday (5 Jumada al-Akhira 1441 AH) Corresponding to (31/1/2020)" (in Arabic), the official website of the Office of His Eminence al-Sayed Ali al-Husseini al-Sistani, https://www.sistani.org/arabic/archive/26381/.

237. "The Text of the Second Sermon Delivered by the Representative of the Supreme Religious Authority, His Eminence Sayed Ahmad Al-Safi, on Friday (12 Jumada al-Akhira 1441 AH) Corresponding to (7/2/2020)" (in Arabic), the official website of the Office of His Eminence al-Sayed Ali al-Husseini al-Sistani, https://www.sistani.org/arabic/archive/26383/.

238. "The Representative of the Supreme Religious Authority Reveals the Reasons for Not Returning the Friday Sermon and Blames the Politicians" (in Arabic), uploaded to the YouTube channel of Al Rabiaa TV (@alrabiaatv) on April 9, 2022, https://www.youtube.com/watch?v=xRGdhuQwVw0.

239. "The Supreme Religious Authority: Medical Instructions Must Be Followed and Applied, and Dealing with the Corona Virus Should Be Done with Caution and Not with Panic and Fear" (in Arabic), the official website of the Al-Abbas Holy Shrine, February 28, 2020, https://alkafeel.net/inspiredfriday/index.php?id=484&ser=2&lang=ar.

240. "The Call of His Eminence's Office to Take Care of Preventive Measures after the Increase in the Number of Infections with the Corona Epidemic in Iraq (6/6/2020)" (in Arabic), the official website of the Office of His Eminence al-Sayed Ali al-Husseini al-Sistani, https://www.sistani.org/arabic/archive/26450/.

241. "The Representative of the Supreme Religious Authority Reveals the Reasons for Not Returning the Friday Sermon and Blames the Politicians" (in Arabic), uploaded to the YouTube channel of Al Rabiaa TV (@alrabiaatv) on April 9, 2022, https://www.youtube.com/watch?v=xRGdhuQwVw0.

242. "His Eminence's Reception of the Special Representative of the Secretary-General of the United Nations (13/9/2020)" (in Arabic), the official website of the Office of His Eminence al-Sayed Ali al-Husseini al-Sistani, https://www.sistani.org/arabic/archive/26461/.

243. Sajad Jiyad, "The Vatican Comes to Najaf, Meeting Power and Piety," *1001 Iraqi Thoughts*, March 6, 2021, https://1001iraqithoughts.com/2021/03/06/the-vatican-comes-to-najaf-meeting-power-and-piety/.

244. "A Statement Issued by His Eminence's Office about His Meeting with the Pope of the Vatican" (in Arabic), the official website of the Office of His Eminence al-Sayed Ali al-Husseini al-Sistani, https://www.sistani.org/arabic/statement/26506/.

245. "Pope Stresses Fraternity in Meeting with Iraq's Grand Ayatollah," *Vatican News*, March 6, 2021, https://www.vaticannews.va/en/pope/news/2021-03/pope-francis-stresses-importance-of-cooperation-fraternity-in-m.html.

246. Jason Horowitz and Jane Arraf, "Pope Francis Meets Iraq's Top Ayatollah as Both Urge Peace," *New York Times*, March 6, 2021, https://www.nytimes.com/2021/03/06/world/europe/pope-francis-iraq-ayatollah-sistani.html.

247. "Pope: Charity, Love and Fraternity Are the Way Forward," *Vatican News*, March 8, 2021, https://www.vaticannews.va/en/pope/news/2021-03/pope-francis-inflight-presser-iraq-journalists0.html.

248. "The Letter of His Eminence to the Supreme Pontiff Pope Francis in Response to His Letter to Him" (in Arabic), the official website of the Office of His Eminence al-Sayed Ali al-Husseini al-Sistani, https://www.sistani.org/arabic/archive/26802/.

249. "Statement of His Eminence's Office on the Upcoming Parliamentary Elections in Iraq" (in Arabic), the official website of the Office of His Eminence al-Sayed Ali al-Husseini al-Sistani, https://www.sistani.org/arabic/statement/26536/.

250. "A Statement by an Official Source in the Office of His Eminence Regarding the Formation of the New Government in Iraq (2/11/2021)" (in Arabic), the official website of the Office of His Eminence al-Sayed Ali al-Husseini al-Sistani, https://www.sistani.org/arabic/archive/26538/.

251. John Davison, "Iraqi Cleric Sadr Calls off Protests after Worst Baghdad Violence in Years," Reuters, August 30, 2022, https://www.reuters.com/world/middle-east/iraq-security-forces-say-four-rockets-land-baghdads-green-zone-2022-08-30/.

252. John Davison, Parisa Hafezi, and Laila Bassam, "How a 92-Year-Old Cleric Silently Halted Iraq's Slide Back into War," Reuters, September 3, 2022, https://www.reuters.com/world/middle-east/how-92-year-old-cleric-silently-halted-iraqs-slide-back-into-war-2022-09-03/.

253. Based on the words of Imam Ali, "There is no opinion for those who are not obeyed."

254. "Statement of His Eminence's Office on the Occasion of Receiving the Under-Secretary-General of the United Nations" (in Arabic), the official website of the Office of His Eminence al-Sayed Ali al-Husseini al-Sistani, https://www.sistani.org/arabic/statement/26646/.

255. "Statement of His Eminence's Office on the Occasion of His Reception of the Head of the United Nations Investigation Team to Promote Accountability for ISIS Crimes" (in Arabic), the official website of the Office of His Eminence al-Sayed Ali al-Husseini al-Sistani, https://www.sistani.org/arabic/statement/26650/.

256. "The Statement Issued by His Eminence's Office on the Earthquake That Hit Turkish and Syrian Territories" (in Arabic), the official website of the Office

of His Eminence al-Sayed Ali al-Husseini al-Sistani, https://www.sistani.org/arabic/
statement/26712/.

257. "A Letter from the Office of His Eminence to the Secretary-General of
the United Nations Regarding the Assault on a Copy of the Holy Qur'an with a
License from the Swedish Police" (in Arabic), the official website of the Office of
His Eminence al-Sayed Ali al-Husseini al-Sistani, https://www.sistani.org/arabic/
statement/26747/.

Chapter 3

1. Official website of the Office of His Eminence al-Sayed Ali al-Husseini
al-Sistani, "Questions of Maktaba Magazine / Hussaini Club in Nabatiya."

2. One member of the opposition related to me his surprise when first meeting Sistani in May 2003 that he had read all the communiques of the various
opposition parties over the past year, had studied their policies in detail, and was
critical of several positions they adopted, as if he was present in all their meetings.

3. "An Open Dialogue with Ayatollah Mujtahid Sayed Riyad Muhammad
Saeed Al-Hakim, Documenting the Years of Ordeal" (in Arabic), Political Prisoners
Foundation, June 20, 2022, https://www.ppf.gov.iq/2022/06/20/24423/

4. In effect, the maraji "elected" Sistani to lead on political matters, which
gives Sistani authority in general affairs, a specific version of wilayat al-faqih that
he adheres to.

5. This also in effect "'elected" Sistani to intervene in political matters; it gave
him authority to speak up on vital issues.

6. His son Muhammad Ridha does this even more widely.

7. Al-Khaffaf, *The Medical Trip of His Eminence al-Sayed al-Sistani and the Najaf
Crisis*, 184.

8. He frequently discusses with his son Muhammad Ridha the best way forward, gaming strategies and challenging assumptions. This is based on my assessment and that of insiders close to Sistani who I have spoken to in the past.

9. It could be argued that there has been a steady attrition of his political
capital, hence his disengagement, and so this strategy has not always worked.

10. Kalantari, *The Clergy and the Modern Middle East*, 7.

11. Abd Al-Razzaq, *Al-Sayed Al-Sistani and His Political Role in Iraq*, 227.

12. "Questions of Associated Press American Agency" (in Arabic), the official
website of the Office of His Eminence al-Sayed Ali al-Husseini al-Sistani, https://
www.sistani.org/arabic/archive/242/.

13. "The Iraqi Chronicle" (in Arabic), Ministry of Justice, issue 4254, October
15, 2012, https://www.moj.gov.iq/uploaded/4254.pdf.

14. Abd al-Hadi al-Hakim, *The Leadership of the Religious Authority of the 1920
Revolution* (Baghdad: Iraqi Ministry of Culture, Tourism and Antiquities, 2022),
509.

15. Khaffaf, *Texts Issued by His Eminence Al-Sayed Al-Sistani on the Iraqi Issue*, 45.

16. Harith Hasan al-Qarawee, "Sistani, Iran, and the Future of Shii Clerical Authority in Iraq," Crown Center for Middle East Studies, Brandeis University, January 2017, https://www.brandeis.edu/crown/publications/middle-east-briefs/pdfs/101-200/meb105.pdf.

17. Marsin Rahim Alshamary, "Religious Peacebuilding in Iraq: Prospects and Challenges from the Hawza," *Journal of Intervention and Statebuilding* 15, no. 4 (2021): 494–509.

18. This is not a term used by Sistani, though several writers such as Abd al-Hadi al-Hakim, who is close to Sistani, have used it frequently.

19. "Questions of the Polish Newspaper *Gazeta Wyborcza*" (in Arabic), the official website of the Office of His Eminence al-Sayed Ali al-Husseini al-Sistani, https://www.sistani.org/arabic/archive/239/.

20. Larry Diamond, *Squandered Victory: The American Occupation and the Bungled Effort to Bring Democracy to Iraq* (New York: Owl Books, 2006), 86.

21. See "Al-Hakim: Al-Jaafari Status Law Was Not Presented in a Timely Manner, and Al-Sistani Did Not Publicly Express His Opinion on It" (in Arabic), *Alsumaria*, December 18, 2013, https://www.alsumaria.tv/news/سياسة/88579/الحكيم-قانون-الأحوال-الجعفري-لم-يطرح-بالوقت-المناسب and https://al-akhbar.com/Opinion/27974.

22. For a comparative view see Babak Rahimi, "Democratic Authority, Public Islam, and Shi'i Jurisprudence in Iran and Iraq: Hussain Ali Montazeri and Ali Sistani" *International Political Science Review* 33, no. 2 (2012): 193–208.

23. From the comments by Abdulaziz Sachedina after meeting with Sistani in August 1998. An archive copy is available at http://ijtihadnet.com/happend-meeting-ayatollah-sistani-sachedina/.

24. Khoei's view of wilayat al-faqih is not as extensive in its theoretical scope of authority and so slightly further from Khomeini's view than Sistani's is.

25. Ali Al-Sistani, *The Rule of No Harm* (Beirut: Dar Al-Moarikh Al-Arabi, 1994), 205. For the full jurisprudential reasoning that Sistani uses to elucidate his view on wilayat al-faqih, including the critique of Khomeini's view, see Ali al-Sistani, *Ijtihad and Taqlid and Ihtiyat* (Jadhafs: Madad for Culture and Media, 2016), 85–129.

26. Mavani, *Religious Authority and Political Thought in Twelver Shi'ism*, 197; and "Queries: Wilayat al-Faqih" (in Arabic), the official website of the Office of His Eminence al-Sayed Ali al-Husseini al-Sistani, https://www.sistani.org/arabic/qa/0755/.

27. Diamond, *Squandered Victory*, 45.

28. See, for example, Alshamary, "Reimagining the Hawza and the State." Sistani has a large following in Iran, several offices and foundations, a large network, and many resources, adding to his caution when dealing with Iranian state.

29. Corboz, "The Najafi Marja'iyya."

30. "Iranian Money in Najaf to Lure Students of the Sistani Seminary" (in Arabic), *Ultra Iraq*, June 25, 2002, https://ultrairaq.ultrasawt.com/خاص-أموال-إيرانية-في-النجف-لإغراء-طلبة-حوزة-السيستاني/العراق-عراق-خاص/سياسة.

31. Qarawee, "Sistani, Iran, and the Future of Shii Clerical Authority in Iraq."

32. This extends to political groups who look to Tehran not Najaf for religious and political guidance. Some of these came as a reaction to perceived negative treatment from Sistani.

33. "A statement by His Eminence Sayed al-Haeri Declaring That He Will Not Continue as a Religious Authority Due to Illness and Advanced Age" (in Arabic), the website of His Eminence Sayed Kadhim Al-Hussaini Al-Haeri, August 29, 2022, https://www.alhaeri.org/pages/statments-detail.php?id=149.

34. An example was Iran wanting Maliki to remain as prime minister in 2014 but having to give up on that after Sistani forced Maliki out.

35. For example, see the recent visit by the head of the seminaries in Iran to Sistani, "Ayatollah Arafi Visits the Grand Ayatollah Sistani in Najaf" (in Arabic), Taghrib News Agency, June 7, 2023, https://www.taghribnews.com/ar/news/595941/اية-الله-اعرافي-يزور-المرجع-السيستاني-في-النجف-الاشرف.

Chapter 4

1. Hassan Abbas, "The Day After al-Sistani," *New Lines Institute*, February 18, 2020, https://newlinesinstitute.org/iran/the-day-after-al-sistani/.

2. Horowitz and Arraf, "Pope Francis Meets Iraq's Top Ayatollah."

3. Thomas L. Friedman, "A Nobel for Sistani," *New York Times*, March 20, 2005, https://www.nytimes.com/2005/03/20/opinion/a-nobel-for-sistani.html.

4. For example, when Sistani underwent surgery in January 2020, both U.S. secretary of state Mike Pompeo and Iranian foreign minister Javad Zarif sent get well messages. See Secretary Pompeo (@SecPompeo), Twitter status update ("Thankful that His Eminence Ayatollah Sistani underwent successful surgery today in #Iraq. My prayers are extended along with the millions of Iraqis to whom he is a source of guidance and inspiration. May God grant him a speedy recovery and long life"), January 17, 2020, https://twitter.com/secpompeo/status/1217988702133280768?s=61&t=11NIo4cGBHBr6FemZVe7dA; and Javad Zarif (@jzarif), Twitter status update January 16, 2020, https://twitter.com/JZarif/status/1217820331231985664?s=20. ("Good news for all of us in Iran and in Iraq of the success of the surgical operation of the great marja, Grand Ayatollah Al-Sayed Ali Al-Sistani, may God perpetuate his abundant shadow. We pray to God Almighty for his speedy recovery and to complete his blessing upon us with his safety.")

5. American officials in the Coalition Provisional Authority and the U.S. government were also critical of Sistani's role in foiling their plans.

6. Two of these politicians, who held key government positions for several years, told me that what they viewed as Sistani's populist tactics, expressed through Friday prayer speeches, were inappropriate interference in political matters.

7. When discussing an issue about extremist Shia preachers with one of the maraji in Najaf in 2013, he told me that he could not do much because everything

is conditional on Sistani acting, and deferring to him on almost every issue has become the default.

8. Several eyewitnesses related this to me, whereby Sistani accepts lavish gifts and then immediately gifts them to others.

9. A recent example is asking for a prayer hall named in his honor to be renamed. See "al-Sistani's Office Demands That His Name Be Removed from the Dar al-Ilm Prayer Hall" (in Arabic), *Shafaqna*, April 9, 2023 https://ar.shafaqna. com/AR/354434/م-اسمه-برفع-يطالب-السيستاني-السيد-مكتب.

10. I asked an aide who accompanied him throughout the trip to give me some insights from Sistani's behavior and he gave the details noted above.

11. He was moved to a house owned by one of his followers in northwest London the next day.

12. While Sistani has kept his Iranian citizenship and turned down several offers to become an Iraqi national, his sons and their families have received Iraqi citizenship.

13. This view may be because some politicians and figures never interacted with Sistani himself and only met Muhammad Ridha or dealt with him via messages. Once, in a visit to Sistani's office in March 2004, I asked Muhammad Ridha a series of religious questions to which he gave verbal answers, but then went to his father to provide written answers.

14. Official website of the Office of His Eminence al-Sayed Ali al-Husseini al-Sistani, "Questions of *Maktaba Magazine* / Hussaini Club in Nabatiya."

15. "Offices of the Marja'iyya" (in Arabic), the official website of the Office of His Eminence al-Sayed Ali al-Husseini al-Sistani, https://www.sistani.org/arabic/data/7/.

16. Among this circle are Ahmad al-Safi, Hussain Aal Yaseen, Muhammad Aal Yahya, Amjad Riyadh, Tariq al-Baghdadi, Izzaldin al-Musawi, Ihsan al-Jawaheri and Nizar Habl al-Matin

17. For example, he is now seen much more regularly in the shrines, at important social occasions, and other events and commemorations. See "Sayed Muhammad Ridha al-Sistani Performs Laylat al-Qadr next to the Master of Martyrs, Peace Be upon Him" (in Arabic), uploaded to YouTube by the channel Shabakat Ashura (@Ahura.network) on April 14, 2023, https://www.youtube.com/ shorts/AfU2IfeodNA; "Sayed Muhammad Ridha al-Sistani Visits the Graves of the Martyrs of the Sufficient Defense" (in Arabic), *Shafaqna*, June 13, 2023, https:// ar.shafaqna.com/AR/367315/ق-يزور-السيستاني-رضا-محمد-السيد-بالصور/; and "The Opening of Sayed al-Sistani's Chapel in the House of Knowledge of Imam al-Khoei in Najaf" (in Arabic), *Shafaqna*, April 6, 2023 https://ar.shafaqna.com/AR/353735/ بالصور؛-افتتاح-مصلى-السيد-السيستاني-ف/.

18. Mehdi Khalaji, "The Last Marja: Sistani and the End of Traditional Religious Authority in Shiism," Washington Institute, September 10, 2006, https:// www.washingtoninstitute.org/policy-analysis/last-marja-sistani-and-end-traditional-religious-authority-shiism.

19. For more on Tusi see Sajad Jiyad, "A Millennium in Najaf: The Hawza of Shaykh Al-Tusi," in *Najaf: Portrait of a Holy City*, ed. Sabrina Mervin, Robert Gleave, and Géraldine Chatelard (Reading: Ithaca Press, 2017), 133–62.

20. Note that most of the senior maraji in Qom are older than Sistani or roughly the same age; in other words, of the same generation.

21. The Shia Endowment laws explicitly mention the authority of the supreme marja'iyya in Najaf.

22. Corboz, "The Najafi Marja'iyya."

23. Shams al-Din al-Waidhi, Muhammad al-Khaqani, Ali Akbar al-Haeri, Alaa al-Din al-Ghuraifi, Muhammad Amin al-Mamaqani, Muhammad al-Sanad, and Muhammad al-Yaqubi are known by the title marja and have some recognition in Najaf, but have small followings and are unlikely to be considered inheritors to the marja'iyya. Qasim al-Taei, Uday al-Assam, Salih al-Taei, and Fadhil al-Budairi are not recognized as maraji.

24. The same applies to inheriting the position of marja among brothers.

25. Abbas Kadhim and Abdullah F. Alrebh, "A Shift Among the Shi'a: Will a Marj'a Emerge from the Arabian Peninsula?," Middle East Institute, January 12, 2021, https://www.mei.edu/publications/shift-among-shia-will-marja-emerge-arabian-peninsula.

26. Aal Radhi is closer to Sistani, his approach to the marja'iyya and his office, and has better political acumen, but Irawani is more popular among the laity and has more students. They may both become maraji, or one could support the other.

27. Muhammad Baqir al-Hakim, Muhammad Sadiq al-Khirsan, Jafar al-Hakim, Muhammad Ali Bahr al-Uloom, Munir al-Khabbaz, are among the ahl al-khibra whose classes are well attended and who are influential in Najaf.

28. The Imam Reza Shrine endowment in Mashhad, Iran can serve as an example of the economic potential of the shrines in Iraq, some estimates of the total assets of that endowment are upwards of $30 billion with annual revenues also in the billions of dollars, see "The Unholy Business Empire of Astan Quds Razavi," *Tehran Bureau*, August 8, 2021, https://tehranbureau.com/the-unholy-business-empire-of-astan-quds-razavi/.

29. "Ayatollah Ashrafi Quoting Sistani: Hawza Students Should Not Be Dependent on Government Salaries" (in Arabic), *Shafaqna*, October 22, 2018, https://iraq.shafaqna.com/AR/130673/إعادة-نشر-آية-الله-الأشرفي-نقلا-عن-السي/.

30. Students can collect stipends from each school or sub-hawza they are enrolled in and from the offices of maraji they are registered with. Not all stipends are of the same amount, but typically students collect around 300,000– 400,000 Iraqi dinars per month (around $200–$275) in total.

31. Abdullah F. Alrebh, "Will Sistani Be the Last Legend? The Challenge of Succession and the Future of the Marj'aiyyah," Middle East Institute, September 28, 2021, https://www.mei.edu/publications/will-sistani-be-last-legend-challenge-succession-and-future-marjaiyyah.

Milton Keynes UK
Ingram Content Group UK Ltd.
UKHW020044210324
439690UK00006B/112